Come on Seabiscuit!

RALPH MOODY

Illustrated by Robert Riger

The kindness of Mrs. Leslie Fenton, formerly Mrs. Charles Howard, in
making available her scrapbooks of Seabiscuit's career is gratefully
acknowledged.

Library of Congress Cataloging-in-Publication Data
Moody, Ralph, 1898–
Come on Seabiscuit! / Ralph Moody; illustrated by Robert Riger.
p.   cm.
Originally published: Boston: Houghton Mifflin Co., 1963.
ISBN 0-8032-8287-7 (pbk.: alk. paper)
1. Seabiscuit (Race horse)   2. Race horses—United States—Biogra-
phy.   3. Horse racing—United States.   I. Title.
SF355.S4 M6   2003
798.4'0092'9—dc21   2002032238

The kindness of Mrs. Leslie Fenton, formerly Mrs. Charles Howard, in making available her scrapbooks of Seabiscuit's career is gratefully acknowledged.

Come on Seabiscuit!

1

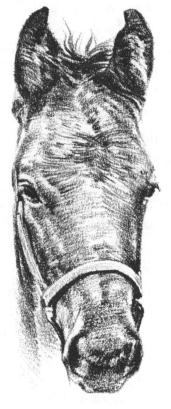

WHEN a son is born into a royal family there is usually rejoicing, particularly if that son may some day become king. But there was no rejoicing when, on May 23, 1933, a son was born into the most distinguished Thoroughbred family in America. The moment the newborn colt lurched awkwardly to his spindly legs, he gave promise of being a disgrace to the family, just as his parents had been.

His father, Hard Tack, was Man o' War's most beautiful son, but had been a failure as a race horse because of his fiery temper and bad behavior. His mother, Swing On, was exactly the opposite. Her father, Whisk Broom II, had sired many of the fastest racers on the American track, but Swing On was a flop-eared, knobby-kneed brown mare, too slow and lazy for racing. Even the colt's color was against him, for he was a solid, muddy bay, with no distinguishing white strip or star on his face.

Both Hard Tack and Swing On were owned by Ogden Mills — Secretary of the United States Treasury — and his sister, Mrs. H. C. Phipps, whose Wheatley racing stable was one of the finest in America. She took tremendous pride in her horses, and spared no expense in their care and training, but insisted that only those be kept which would bring honor to her stable. If Hard Tack and Swing On had not been of royal ancestry, they would have been sold as discards when they proved worthless as racers, but there is an axiom in racing circles that "blood will tell," that when descendants of two great racing families are mated their offspring is apt to have amazing speed. So the two failures were retired to Claiborne Farm in the heart of the Kentucky bluegrass country, the most aristocratic Thoroughbred nursery in the land, and there their son was foaled.

Because his father was Hard Tack — the hard biscuit of the sea — the colt was named Seabiscuit. But Noah, groom at the foaling stable, was unimpressed when Seabiscuit arrived. He shuffled to the office and reported, "Mr. Hancock, sir, Swing On done had her foal, but he sure don't look like he goin' to 'mount to much. Too big in he head, too short in he legs, and he got them same knobby knees like he mammy. Runty little thing; reckon he goin' be 'nother Swing On."

Claiborne Farm is one of the most beautiful of all horse nurseries. Its meadows, separated by white board fences, stretch across mile after mile of gently rolling hills, deep in bluegrass, and shaded by groves of hardwood. The stables are horse palaces, surrounded by paddocks, stallion runs, weaning pens, and training strips, each enclosed by an immaculate

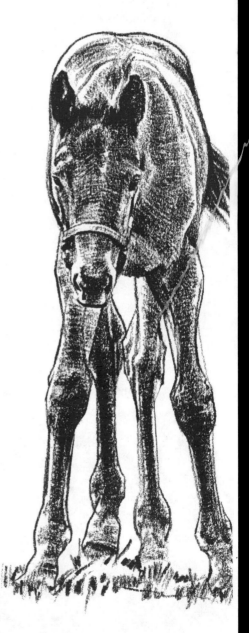

white fence. There, in spacious stalls knee-deep with fresh straw, nearly a hundred foals are born in a single year. They are never thrown together in large herds, but separated into small classes, like children at a private school. Seabiscuit and Swing On were put into a fifty-acre pasture with nine other Thoroughbred mares and their newborn foals.

Colts are much like children, and their first year is their kindergarten. Each class is chosen with the greatest care, for the colts will remain together through their second summer, and must be as evenly matched as possible in age and ability. All Thoroughbred foals are born with the urge to run, so much of their play at pasture is a series of spontaneous races. And

nothing builds as strong racing muscles, or awakens a colt's competitive spirit more than these games he plays at pasture.

In every group of colts, as in every group of boys, there are usually two who stand out from all the others. One is the hero; endowed with far more than his share of good looks, size, cleverness, and speed. Another is the outcast: an awkward, runty little fellow, looking as if he might have slipped in under the gate when no one was watching. Seabiscuit was the outcast in his class, and Granville was the hero.

Granville was taller, more finely built, more spirited, and faster than the others. A dozen times a day he would fling up his bushy tail, nicker, and race away across the pasture. Close behind him ran Snark and Flares, with the others bunched at their heels, and knobby-kneed Seabiscuit pounding along in the rear. It would have discouraged almost any other colt, but not Seabiscuit. He didn't know the meaning of discouragement. The farther he was left behind the harder he drove himself, and the longer the race the nearer he came to catching up.

Seabiscuit was champion of his class in only one respect: he had the biggest appetite. With his big head and short, spindly legs, he had to spend more energy than the other colts in running, and it required more food to replace that energy. Even with his big appetite, he grew more slowly than his playmates, but because he had to work harder at his running than they, he developed stronger, tougher leg muscles and sinews. By late fall he was no longer straggling at the tail end of the pack, but running with Snark and Flares, close on the heels of Granville.

During the winter Seabiscuit and his classmates had their own quarters at the stables, with a large paddock where they could run and play on warm days. There they all celebrated their birthday on January 1, 1934, for Thoroughbred foals, regardless of the date on which they are born, become yearlings on their first New Year's Day. By early spring most of the colts were nearly as tall as their mothers, and when they shed their shaggy winter coats they emerged as beautiful little race horses. But Seabiscuit was the exception, and looked more like a ragged range pony than a Thoroughbred, for he had failed to shed his winter coat, and his legs and back were two or three inches shorter than the average. He was so much the ugly duckling on Claiborne Farm that when Mrs. Phipps came there in April to look over her yearlings, he was hidden away in an outlying barn.

Although Seabiscuit was the smallest and least beautiful of his class, he was no longer the straggler when the yearlings were turned out to pasture. In their first race he swept past Snark and Flares, forcing Granville to lay back his ears and run his best to stay in front. By the time the runt had shed his winter coat, Granville could barely stay in front of him, and a fierce rivalry sprang up between them, for whatever Seabiscuit lacked in physical equipment he more than made up for in stamina and determination. By midsummer the rivals were racing neck-and-neck, and Seabiscuit formed a habit that would mark him for the rest of his life. Whenever they were bulldogging for the lead he would snort at Granville, scolding him and trying to throw him off pace. No one can say what the outcome of the rivalry between Seabiscuit and Granville might have been if they had remained at pasture for another year, but a race horse's training for the track begins at the end of his second summer. In training, the outcome was nearly ruinous for Seabiscuit.

The horse is one of our most intelligent animals, but no horse has the intelligence to develop himself to the peak of his ability. In Thoroughbred racing circles it is claimed, and justly so, that for every race

Robert Rider

won at least as much credit belongs to the trainer and jockey as to the horse himself. For this reason, wealthy owners contract, year after year, for the services of the most successful jockeys and trainers — and "Sunny Jim" Fitzsimmons was recognized as the most successful trainer of Thoroughbreds in America. So, since Seabiscuit and Granville each belonged to a very wealthy stable, they were shipped to Fitzsimmons for training when brought in from pasture. No finer choice of trainers could have been made for Granville but, quite probably, no worse could have been made for Seabiscuit.

Fitzsimmons had trained the fathers of both colts, and any man is inclined to judge a son by his knowledge of the youngster's father. Sunny Jim's knowledge was, to say the least, unfortunate for Seabiscuit, and it made Granville his highly prized favorite on first sight.

Granville's father was Gallant Fox, perfectly behaved, winner of the coveted Triple Crown — the Kentucky Derby, the Preakness, and the Belmont Stakes — and the horse which had earned Fitzsimmons his greatest fame as a trainer. Hard Tack had earned little more than Sunny Jim's everlasting hatred. He had been an outlaw when sent for training as a yearling, and no amount of careful handling would break him of his vicious habits. There was no doubt that he could run faster than most colts, but his natural speed could never be developed because he fought wildly against every attempt to train him. When he became a five-year-old, the famous trainer had refused to waste any more time on him. Beyond that, Fitz had given up on Swing On when he found her too slow and lazy to be worth training.

It is not surprising that when Seabiscuit and Granville arrived, one should have been looked upon as a blessing and the other as a curse. Granville was beautiful, well-mannered, alert, and an almost exact duplicate of his famous father in size and conformation. Seabiscuit had only the reputation of his infamous father, and in appearance was almost the exact duplicate of his knobby-kneed, lazy mother. Sunny Jim can hardly be blamed for deciding that Granville was by far the superior of the two colts and must be handled with the utmost care and consideration, while Seabiscuit must be compelled to accept training. The decision proved to be one of the few times the great trainer misjudged a horse and it barely missed being completely disastrous to Seabiscuit.

A clash of personalities between two strong-willed humans is not uncommon, but it is amazing when so deep-seated a clash develops between a man and a horse as that between Fitzsimmons and Seabiscuit. Fitz was determined that he would force the yearling to give him his best efforts, and Seabiscuit was equally determined that he would not be forced. He was too intelligent to fight wildly, as his father had, but the stronger the pressure put on him the less he would cooperate, and the more determinedly he refused to turn on his speed.

Only once was Seabiscuit's determination broken, and then it was from fright and panic rather than intention. He had been tried in workouts with Faust, the fastest sprinter among the yearlings, but no matter how much his jockey urged him, he wouldn't try to make a race of it. Finally, Fitz became exasperated. One morning he picked up a stout stick, passed it to the jockey, and told him, "Hit Seabiscuit just as many times as you can in a quarter-mile, and keep him as close as you can to Faust."

The jockey carried out the first half of his instructions with all his might, but couldn't do much about the second half. In trying to escape the severe beating, Seabiscuit left Faust far behind, and ran the quarter-mile in twenty-two and two-fifths seconds. This was probably the fastest quarter-mile ever run by a yearling colt carrying a jockey, but it did Seabiscuit more harm than good, for it convinced Sunny Jim Fitzsimmons that he would do his best only under severe punishment. The rest of Seabiscuit's yearling season was hardly a happy time for either himself or his trainer.

Owners of race horses generally follow the recommendation of the trainer in deciding whether or not a colt is worthy to remain in their stable, and the decision is usually made at the end of the yearling's training season. When, on January 1, 1935, the yearlings in training under Jim Fitzsimmons became two-year-olds, Seabiscuit was tossed into the discard, while Granville became the pampered favorite.

At that time Fitzsimmons moved his training stable to Florida for the winter racing season. There the training of Granville and the other well-regarded two-year-olds was carried on with the greatest care and patience, in order to prepare them for their all-important three-year-old campaigns. But Seabiscuit was put to work. On January 19 he was entered in a short race, and trailed the winner to the wire by four and a half lengths. This loss was enough for Fitz; he was surer than ever that he wanted no more to do with the obstinate son of Hard Tack. He gave Seabiscuit only two days of rest, then entered him in a $2500 claiming race.

Thoroughbred race horses are not advertised generally for sale, as is the case with most other animals, but are entered in claiming races. These are races where a selling price is established in advance, and any horse entered may be claimed and bought at that price. Even though Seabiscuit finished second in the race and the price was ridiculously low for a grandson of Man o' War, no one claimed him. Sunny Jim was too well known, and other horsemen reasoned that he wouldn't be trying to get rid of the colt at that price unless those knobby knees were on the verge of breaking down. Jim tried again, five days later and at the same price, but still there was no claimer.

When we go to the races and see the Thorough-breds streaking around the track, they appear almost to be flying, for they never have more than two feet on the ground, and then only for a twentieth of a second in each stride. All the rest of the time they are either airborne, or supported by a single leg. To carry a light jockey at this gait looks to be a much easier task than that of a horse pulling a heavy load, but it is exactly the opposite.

The average Thoroughbred race horse weighs more than half a ton, carries a load well over a hundred pounds, leaps twenty feet or farther at each stride, and lands with the entire weight on one front leg. The strain on the bones, tendons, and joints of that leg is tremendous, and the faster the pace the greater the landing impact becomes. Beyond this, the energy required for each twenty-foot leap is equal to that ex-pended by a horse pulling a half-ton load five times as far, and in a mile race a horse must take more than two hundred and sixty such leaps.

Even a fully matured and well-trained horse will break down under the strain unless given sufficient rest between hard races. A twenty-months-old colt is almost certain to, for his bones are not yet hard enough, or his tendons strong enough to withstand the incessant impact on pasterns, ankles, and knees. For this reason, immature Thoroughbreds are usually raced sparingly, but before Seabiscuit was twenty-four months old, Fitzsimmons had raced him thirteen times.

In comparison, Man o'War was raced only twenty-one times in his entire life.

Four of the races in which Seabiscuit had been entered were $2500 claiming races, but no owner would risk even so small an amount on a colt that had already been raced enough to ruin him forever. His other nine races had all been for low purses, but against poor enough competition that he had earned $650 in second-, third-, and fourth-place prizes. It then became evident that Fitz had given up hope of the colt's being claimed at any price, and decided to make a workhorse of him; using him as a training mate for more highly regarded colts, and entering him in every race where there was the slightest possibility that he might earn a few more dollars before his racing days were over.

In late May Seabiscuit was taken to Rockingham Park at Salem, New Hampshire, and entered in five races within a period of three weeks, but regardless of how hard he was whipped, did no better than second against mediocre competition. He was then taken to Narragansett Park in Rhode Island for three races. In the first of these he was matched against better colts than before, and was not expected to make much of a showing, so his jockey didn't try to force him. That was all that was necessary. Seabiscuit romped to the wire, winner for his first time on a race track, and by two full lengths. In hope of making a good sale while the memory of the win was still fresh in other horsemen's minds, Sunny Jim immediately entered him in a $4000 claiming race. Again the colt's jockey let him run as he pleased, and in appreciation he broke the track record, streaking under the wire two lengths in the lead, and winning $2795.

Still, no horseman dared risk the claiming price on a colt that had been so obviously overworked, so Sunny Jim put him back to still harder work. Between September 2d and October 2d, he was raced six times on four different tracks. In the last of these races Seabiscuit was so worn down, and the strain on his knees had become so great, that he finished last — ten lengths behind the winner. Fitzsimmons had little choice but to give him two weeks' rest. Then he was entered in the Springfield Handicap at Agawam, in the hope that he might yet win a few more dollars. He did. He set another track record, and earned $2030.

Still not satisfied with his "failure" colt, Sunny Jim entered Seabiscuit a week later in the Ardsley Handicap at the Empire City track — and again the knobby-kneed colt broke the track record, as well as earning another $2835. As though this weren't enough, he was moved back to Rhode Island three days later, and run in the Pawtucket Handicap. The best he could do there was to take second place and win $1000. The next time out, on November 11, the courageous colt was so nearly broken down that he finished six lengths behind the winner.

In that first season Seabiscuit, the outcast nobody

wanted, had run in thirty-five races, set three track records, and earned a total of $12,510. To fill in spare time he had been used as training mate for Granville, but that pampered favorite's record as a two-year-old had been somewhat less impressive. Granville had been entered 'in just seven races, had won only one, and earned a total of $1525. But he was still the favorite — and Seabiscuit was the outcast.

When, at the end of 1935, Fitzsimmons again moved his stable to Florida for the winter season, Seabiscuit was too exhausted and worn out to be raced. He was thin and listless, plodded along like a plowhorse, and swung his left foreleg sideways as he walked, a sure sign that the knee was painfully injured. His knobby knees were the weakest part of his body, and would probably have broken down completely if it had not been for his extreme intelligence and courage.

A race horse must lead with his left (inside) foreleg when rounding the ends of the track. Otherwise he is very apt to stumble and fall. The leading foreleg is the second to strike the ground when a galloping horse lands from his leap. Beside bearing the entire weight, it is the pivot on which he turns, and supplies the spring for his next leap. The twisting strain on tendons, ankles, and knee is terrific. There is little doubt that Seabiscuit's left knee would have been damaged beyond any possibility of healing if it had not been for a trick he learned in his first few grueling races. Just before and after each curve, he would take a

17

skipping step, so as to lead with his right foreleg on straightaways and save his left for the turns.

In Florida, Seabiscuit was allowed a short rest, then given the most heartbreaking task imaginable. Fitzsimmons had spared Granville any possible strain as a two-year-old, and was preparing him to follow in his illustrious father's footsteps as a three-year-old — the winning of the Triple Crown. To get him ready for the campaign, not only his speed, but his competitive spirit must be sharpened to a keen edge, and Seabiscuit was used as the grindstone.

The rivalry that had sprung up between the two colts in their pasture days had never cooled. Although Seabiscuit refused to be forced into running his best, he needed no forcing when matched with Granville on the training track, but drove himself fiercely in his determination to win. And whenever they were bulldogging shoulder-to-shoulder for the lead, he would look Granville in the eye and snort his challenge. But Granville always won — and for one reason only. He might become discouraged if he were beaten, and no such risk could be taken with a colt that was being prepared to win the Triple Crown, so Seabiscuit was always pulled up just before reaching the finish wire.

Nothing is so damaging to a race horse's competitive spirit as being held back and kept from winning. But Seabiscuit was no ordinary race horse. Instead of becoming discouraged, he became angry, irritable, and more determined than ever. Although he had been gentle and affectionate at Claiborne Farm, he became unruly, bad tempered, and developed the habit of walking around and around his stall to let off steam.

In April Granville was shipped to Louisville for the Kentucky Derby, and Seabiscuit was put back to the grind of racing. Because of his weakened knee, he no longer ran in a straight, true line, but lugged in toward the rail, making him unfit for first-class races. But by the end of July he had been entered in ten cheap handicap and purse races — on five different tracks, and in four states. He won a couple of them against poor competition, but in others he finished as much as ten lengths behind, and no amount of whipping would make him put out his best effort.

Fitzsimmons had not entered Seabiscuit in a claiming race for more than a year, but on August 3, 1936, he entered him in the $6000 Mohawk Claiming Stakes at Saratoga. There had been nothing in the colt's three-year-old showing to indicate that he might win, but he did — by six full lengths, and for $2960.

It might almost seem that Seabiscuit sensed its being a claiming race, and that he ran his best in hope that some other horseman would claim him. He wasn't claimed, but that race was the pivot on which his fortunes turned. Up in the stands an old-time cowboy had seen and recognized what Jim Fitzsimmons had never been able to recognize — the heart, courage, and determination that marked the gallant colt as a truly great horse. The cowboy turned to a man beside him — a man who had once said he wouldn't pay five dollars for the best horse in the country — and said, "Get me that horse, Mr. Howard. He's got real stuff in him. I can improve him, I'm positive."

A week later Seabiscuit was bought by Charles S. Howard, of California, for $8000, and turned over to Tom Smith, the old-time cowboy, for handling and training.

2

THE RAILBIRDS nearly split their sides with laughing when the news was circulated that Charles Howard had bought Seabiscuit, and that old Tom Smith had said he could improve the colt. Nothing could have seemed more ridiculous. Who was this man Howard, and what did he know about race horses? He must be out of his mind if he thought an old-time cowboy could improve a horse that had been trained by Sunny Jim Fitzsimmons — the man who had developed two of the only three horses in history ever to win the Triple Crown. Poor Seabiscuit! He was on the skids for sure, but what difference? Those weak knees of his wouldn't hold up for more than another race or two anyway. If they would, smart old Sunny Jim would never have let the colt go. The railbirds would have laughed still louder if they had known who Seabiscuit's jockey would be.

As a young man Charles Howard had opened a little bicycle repair shop in San Francisco. That was before there were any garages, so the few people who owned automobiles took them to the bicycle shop when they needed repairing. Most of the very early automobiles in San Francisco were "two lunger" Buicks, so it was only natural that young Howard should become the Buick agent in the city.

When, after the great San Francisco earthquake and fire, automobiles began replacing carriage horses, Charles Howard's business began to boom. He was selling Buicks faster than he could get them shipped from Detroit to the West Coast. When he doubled his orders, the company cautioned him that he might find himself overstocked, since most people still preferred the driving horse to the automobile.

Young as he was, Charles Howard was already a keen, farsighted businessman. He wrote back, "I must have the cars I have ordered as fast as you can get them here. The day of the horse is past, and the people in San Francisco want automobiles. I wouldn't give five dollars for the best horse in this country."

Wrong as he later proved himself to be about what he would pay for the best horse in the country, his foresight regarding automobiles was keen and accurate. Because of it, he became a multimillionaire, and the biggest automobile distributor on the West Coast. He bought a beautiful ranch in the redwood country of northern California, stocked it with excellent ponies when his sons proved to be fine polo players, and became prominent in California horse circles.

Late in 1933 pari-mutuel wagering on horse races was legalized in California, and as a result, several of the finest racing establishments in the world were built in the state. The cost of building a racing plant is enormous, and the money is usually furnished by very wealthy men who have a love for horses. Charles Howard had both the love for horses and the wealth, so was one of the Californians to finance the famous Santa Anita track. With his large investment in a race track, it was only natural that he should become interested in Thoroughbred race horses, and should decide to establish a racing stable. But he knew very little about Thoroughbreds, and there were no famous trainers in California, such as Sunny Jim Fitzsimmons. Tom Smith, the man Mr. Howard chose as his advisor and trainer, was about the most unlikely one imaginable.

"Silent Tom" Smith was fifty-seven years old when a friend sent him to Charles Howard to ask for a job as horse trainer. He was a quiet, dead-broke, little man, and his only education had been received in the school of hard knocks. When he was six, his family had moved from Georgia to Texas, and he had grown up in a saddle. Then, when he was thirteen, he had worked with a professional horsebreaker. Learning to ride wild broncos could hardly be expected to fit a boy to become a trainer of Thoroughbred horses, but Tom Smith not only learned to ride outlaw horses, he learned to understand them — and he never stopped learning.

By the time Tom became twenty-one he was a top-notch cowboy, and had gained a reputation that was rare, even in Texas. It was claimed that he could keep the upper hand with any animal, and that no horse had ever been known to get the better of him. Because he preferred to work alone and had little to say when with other men, he was given the name of Silent Tom, and it was believed that he had a secret about controlling animals which he wouldn't tell. He did have a secret, and he wouldn't tell it for fear he might be ridiculed. From the time he was a boy, he had believed that animals reacted the same as people did, that whenever one became an outlaw or misbehaved there was a cause for it, and that the fault could be corrected if the cause were discovered. The reason for his preferring to work alone was that he could study the causes better in that way. And the reason for his silence was that the communication between men and animals must be through understanding, not conversation.

With the outbreak of the Boer War in 1899, the British government sent agents to the United States to buy fifty thousand cavalry horses. There was only one place where any such a number of horses suitable for cavalry use could be found; in the wild mustang herds that roamed the prairies of Texas, Colorado, Wyoming, and Montana. The Moncrief brothers went into the business of catching and breaking these wild horses, offering to pay seventy-five dollars a month for cowboys who would tackle the rough and dangerous job. That was more than twice what Tom Smith was making as a cowhand, and exactly the kind of a job he liked, so he hired out to the Moncriefs as a horsebreaker. Until the order was filled, he often rode as many as thirty bucking horses in a single day — and from every one of them he learned to understand horses a little better.

After working for the Moncriefs Tom didn't return to Texas, but took a job as foreman on the Unaweep Cattle Range at Grand Junction, Colorado. In those days the foreman on a big cattle ranch had to be veterinarian, horse trainer, and often blacksmith, as well as bossing the cowhands and planning the roundups. Tom Smith went at his foreman's job in the same way he had gone at horsebreaking — by studying it out instead of guessing, and by listening instead of talking. In Grand Junction there was a livery stable owner named Guy Bedwell, who was a great talker, and who later became the greatest Thoroughbred trainer of his time. Like all great talkers, the people he liked best were those who were good listeners, and "Silent Tom" Smith was one of the best.

Whenever the crew from the Unaweep Range rode

into town for a Saturday night blowout, Tom spent his time at Bedwell's livery stable, listening and learning. And in appreciation, Guy Bedwell taught him many of the tricks of the training art: how to shoe a horse so as to correct the faults in its gait; how to build its running muscles, fire a bowed tendon, bandage and treat a sprained joint, mix his own liniments and medicines, balance a diet, and a hundred other little tricks that are known only by an expert trainer.

The close friendship between Tom and Guy continued until 1906, when Bedwell sold his livery stable and went on to become the most renowned Thoroughbred trainer of that period. For another fifteen years Tom stayed on the Unaweep Range as foreman, but he never forgot a lesson he had learned from his friend Bedwell, and he never forgot his yearning to become a trainer of Thoroughbreds himself.

Tom Smith was forty-three years old before he had his first chance to try his hand as a trainer of Thoroughbreds — and it wasn't much of a chance. In 1921 the owners of the ranch sold out, and Tom found a job as foreman with McCarty and Landrum. Their business was that of furnishing bucking broncos for small rodeos throughout the West. They also had a half dozen Thoroughbreds that they shipped along with the broncos, for putting on relay races. Every one of them was an abused and broken-down old race horse, worth less than a hundred dollars. One or two were seemingly hopeless outlaws, and all the others had sprained knees, cracked hoofs, bowed tendons, or broken wind. But they were Thoroughbreds, the horses Tom Smith had yearned to handle and train for more than twenty years, and he went to work on them as carefully as though each one had been a Triple Crown winner.

Through understanding, patience, and patchwork, Tom improved his half dozen old has-beens until they were winning far more than their share of the races at the little bush-circuit rodeos. His success with them brought him to the attention of "Cowboy Charlie" Irwin, of the Irwin Livestock and Show Company. Cowboy Charlie was then promoting and furnishing horses — both bucking and racing — for frontier shows in every part of the West, from the Missouri River to the Pacific Coast, and from Canada to Mexico. His horses were of about the same quality as those owned by McCarty and Landrum, but he was a big operator, and had many more of them — sometimes as many as fifty racers. What he needed badly was a man who could keep them patched up enough to race after taking the punishment of being shipped from town to town in boxcars, and Tom Smith proved to be exactly the right man.

For more than ten years Tom worked as foreman for Cowboy Charlie Irwin, constantly on the move from one frontier show to another, and constantly patching up the broken-down old nags that were put into his care. It isn't at all strange that, with so much practice, he became the best horse patcher in the business. But Tom Smith was never satisfied with doing only a patchwork job. He studied every Thoroughbred turned over to him as carefully as though it had been worth a thousand times its cost. His first care was to gain an understanding between himself and the horse. Then he set about healing its injuries as much as they could be healed, correcting its faults when they could be corrected, strengthening its body through proper feeding and training, and rekindling its determination to win.

Each year Tom became more successful as a trainer of broken-down race horses, and each year the old has-beens entrusted to his care won more and more races. But with the coming of the big depression in the early 1930's, Cowboy Charlie's show business ran into hard times. There were months when he couldn't pay Tom's wages, small as they were, but money was of little interest to Silent Tom. He became obsessed with a love and admiration for Thoroughbred race horses, and his greatest joy in life was to rebuild the ones that other men had discarded as hopeless. Whether or not he was paid made little difference to him, so long as he could have the feed, medicines, and supplies that his horses needed.

During the World's Fair at Chicago, Tom reached the top as a bush-league horse trainer. At that time a nine-day rodeo was held at Soldiers Field, just outside the Fair Grounds, and Tom's patched-up old racers won sixteen of the eighteen racing events. Then Cowboy Charlie Irwin was killed in an automobile accident — and Tom Smith was out of a job. Pari-mutuel wagering on horse races had just been legalized in California, and racing was becoming a popular sport, so Tom went there to look for a job. He had been there only a short time when a friend told him, "Charlie Howard, the wealthy Buick man, bought seventeen Thoroughbred yearlings at Saratoga lately, and he needs a trainer for them. Why don't you go and see if you can get the job?"

Tom got the job of training the yearlings — and more. He won the complete confidence and trust of his new boss. Mr. Howard took him East to see what they could pick up in the way of a few inexpensive Thoroughbreds; horses that could be raced on the new California tracks until the yearlings would be ready in a year or two. They had looked at scores of Thoroughbreds before Tom saw Seabiscuit run in the Mohawk Claiming Stakes, recognized his quality, courage, and determination at a glance, and told his boss, "Get me that horse. I can improve him."

Mr. Howard was going to Detroit from New York, so Seabiscuit was taken along in order that Tom might study him and, if he thought best, try him out in a race or two there. It didn't require much study for Tom to find out that the colt was extremely intelligent, and that his misbehavior was due to pain, frustration, and exhaustion. He had long ago discovered that highly intelligent horses reacted exactly the same as highly intelligent people. When overworked, in pain, frustrated, and physically exhausted, they lost their appetites, and their nervous systems became upset, making them irritable and resentful of any attempt to force them.

Seabiscuit's lack of appetite and continual walking in his stall were positive proof that his nerves were on edge. He laid his ears back, snapped, and threatened to attack whenever a groom went into his stall. He hung back and sulked when taken out for his morning exercise, was unruly at the starting gate, and fought against any restraint or urging when on the track. Tom set about to correct these bad habits by removing the cause, rather than by the use of force.

Tom had decided to make the colt's first workout a slow canter, just enough to give him a little exercise. But Seabiscuit decided to show his resentment of restraint by making it into a runaway. Tom let him run — for a full two miles. There isn't much fun in fighting against a man who won't fight back, and there isn't much chance to show resentment against restraint when there isn't any. After his two-mile runaway, Seabiscuit came to the conclusion that it was senseless and a waste of energy to fight against his new trainer. He behaved himself on the way back to the barn, and by the time he had been cooled out he was hungry enough that he was glad to take a carrot from Tom's hand.

When a person who is nervous and upset is left alone, he will brood about his troubles, and the more he broods the more irritable and disagreeable he will become. But if he has company, he is less inclined to think about himself and the injustices that have been done him. Then too, even though we don't particularly want something that we have, we dislike having someone else try to take it away from us. In boyhood, Tom Smith had noticed that animals had these same traits, so he tried an experiment on Seabiscuit. He put a nanny goat in the stall with him. Just having company was enough to stop the nervous colt from his continual stall walking. The goat was a curiosity to him, and except for its greediness, they might have become good friends.

Although Seabiscuit had been a heavy feeder before he was put to racing, his appetite had decreased as the strain on his nerves and the pain of his injured knee had increased. He had become a nibbler and a picker, but there was nothing the matter with Nanny's appetite. At feeding time she climbed right atop the forkful of hay, trying to stow it all away before Seabiscuit could get any. Even though he wasn't hungry, he had no intention of letting her hog the whole meal, so for a couple of feedings he tried to get his share. But Nanny was just too greedy to be put up with. When she climbed onto the next forkful, Seabiscuit picked her up by the scruff of the neck. Holding her firmly in his teeth, he walked once around the stall, giving her a good shaking, then set her down outside the doorway where a groom could rescue her.

Though Tom's goat experiment hadn't been entirely successful, it had done the two things he was most anxious for. It had shown that with a companion in the stall Seabiscuit's nerves would quiet enough to keep him from his continual walking, and that, with a little competition, his appetite-could be stimulated. The next task was to find him the best possible stall companion, and Tom didn't have much trouble in doing it.

At all race tracks there are ponies which are used for leading fractious Thoroughbreds to the starting gate. They are usually little fellows, not worth very much, and their greatest requirement is that they be gentle and friendly, so as to quiet the horse that is being led. At the Fair Grounds track in Detroit there was a little palomino lead pony, named Pumpkin because of his golden color. He was nine years old, and not much of a horse, but he was gentle and friendly with other horses, so when Seabiscuit tossed the goat out, Tom Smith put Pumpkin into a double stall with him. Within an hour he and Seabiscuit had formed a friendship that lasted the rest of their lives, and the war of nerves was nearly won. Seabiscuit quit his habit of stall walking entirely, his appetite became much better, and with it his disposition improved remarkably. He seemed to sense that he was no longer an outcast, but among friends, and his resentment of handling was rapidly forgotten.

Whatever part of Seabiscuit's irritability wasn't cured by understanding treatment, and his companionship with Pumpkin, was taken care of by Silent Tom's skill as a veterinarian and his years of experience in patching up broken-down race horses. He devised braces for the colt's sprained ankle and knee; flexible enough that he could walk with them on, but strong enough to take the strain off as he stood in his stall, so as to relieve him of the constant, irritating pain. Since both knees and ankles had been weakened by overwork as a two-year-old, Tom rubbed them with a soothing liniment after every workout, put braces on them, padded them heavily with cotton, and bandaged all four legs from below the ankles to above the knees and hocks. One sports writer said in his column that "Smith's bandages look like World War One puttees," but they did the trick, strengthened the weakened joints, and worked wonders on Seabiscuit's disposition.

While Tom Smith was in Detroit, getting acquainted with Seabiscuit and discovering ways to correct his bad habits, two other down-and-out horsemen were making their way there for the races at the Fair Grounds, but their luck seemed to have run out. One of them was Jim Allen, known around the race tracks as Yummy. He was a jockey's agent, but most of the boys he represented were small-time riders, there was a depression on, and Yummy had been barely making a living. He was driving one of his riders to Detroit, in hope of finding him a few mounts to ride in the races, when his auto was wrecked in a collision. Both boys were badly shaken up, but they managed to hitch-hike their way to the city. They reached the Fair Grounds a couple of days after Tom Smith got there with Seabiscuit, and between them they had $7.60 and two soiled shirts.

The jockey that Yummy brought to Detroit was Jack Pollard, known at the small-time race tracks of the West as "Red," and in the smaller-time boxing rings at the Frontier shows and carnivals as "The Cougar." Red Pollard was born in Alberta, Canada, in 1909. Ever since he became seventeen he had been kicking around the West — riding any race horse he could get to ride, and boxing any bantam-weight who dared to get into a ring with him. His love for Thoroughbreds was as deep as Tom Smith's, but the ones he'd had a chance to ride were mostly of the same type as those Tom had been training. Although Red was one of the better jockeys on the bush circuit, he had won only three stake races in his life.

When the boys reached the Fair Grounds, Yummy took Red from trainer to trainer, trying to find him a horse to ride. He'd take anything, even an outlaw, just to earn a few dollars for room rent and grub. There were more jockeys than jobs, and every horse in every race had been spoken for. Yummy had been to every trainer he knew, and to nearly every barn on the Fair Grounds, when a groom told him, "There's a new trainer here; one nobody never heard of before — a guy that won't do no talking. He fetched a gimpy colt out here from Saratoga a couple of days ago. I hear tell it belongs to some automobile man from out to California. Don't know if they're going to try racing the colt — he's a bad actor — but they've got him over in the east barn. Why don't you go see the guy? His name's Smith. You might pick the kid up a job as exercise boy."

It was late afternoon when Yummy and Red found the barn where Seabiscuit was stabled. Tom had bandaged the colt's legs for the night, and, as was his custom when getting acquainted with a new horse, was sitting just outside the stall doorway. He still had a lot of thinking and planning to do, and as he did it he was enjoying the afternoon sunshine — his camp chair leaned back against the barn, his battered old hat pulled down over his forehead, dark glasses protecting his eyes, and chewing the end of a straw. He was so busy with his thoughts that he didn't notice the two boys coming toward him until Yummy called out, "Good afternoon, Mr. Smith. I hear you've got a horse you might be needing a good jockey for. I've got one of the best in the business here. I want you to meet . . ."

Tom took the straw out of his mouth, grinned, and cut in, "You don't have to introduce me to The

Cougar. We knowed each other on the leaky-roof circuit, when times was real tough."

"They're still tough," Red told him.

Tom Smith paid no more attention to Yummy, but told Red, "I've got a horse here named Seabiscuit. A better one than anybody thinks. I need a strong boy to handle him — one that's kicked around like you and me, and knows how to get along with the stove-up ones. You take a look at him, work him a little and we'll see."

It is well known that some men are exceptionally keen in their judgment of a horse. It is not so well known that exceptionally intelligent horses are equally good judges of men. They can tell from a man's scent whether he is afraid or assured, nervous or calm, rough or gentle, and above all, whether or not he is worthy of their trust and confidence.

Seabiscuit and Pumpkin were munching hay at the far side of the box stall when Red Pollard went to the doorway and leaned on the closed half-door. Pumpkin paid no attention, but Seabiscuit raised his head, turned it toward the doorway, and sniffed. For a minute he stood, sampling the scent of the boy whose head and shoulders showed above the half-door. What he read in that scent seemed to satisfy him. He left his hay, and came over to rub his muzzle against Red's shoulder.

There was no need for Charles Howard or Tom Smith to make any decision as to who their jockey would be; Seabiscuit had made the decision for himself. He stood, still rubbing his muzzle on the shoulder, while Red Pollard stroked his neck and told him, "We're goin' places together, Baby, you and me. There ain't nobody goin' to stop us — not nobody."

It was just soft-talk — the kind a man will talk to a horse he has fallen in love with — but Red believed it, and though Seabiscuit couldn't understand the words, he seemed to believe it too. When Tom Smith came to join them, the colt stood nuzzling them both. He had found the two men he trusted, the two men he wanted to please, and from that day he gave them the best he had. And they gave him all he had ever needed: understanding, painstaking care, and affection.

3

In no horse can the results of nearly two years of abuse and overwork be cured in a single day, week, or month. And some of those results can never be entirely cured. If Red Pollard's prediction that Seabiscuit and he would go places were to come true, the task before the bush-league trainer and jockey seemed impossible, but they went at it as though they had no doubt of their success. With any lesser horse than Seabiscuit, considering the abuse he had suffered, it would have been completely impossible, for boundless courage, limitless stamina, a heart too great to falter, and an indomitable will to win cannot be put into any horse. He must be born with them. Men can only develop and sharpen what is already there, but the job that Tom Smith and Red Pollard did stands alone in American Thoroughbred history.

With Tom planning each move and giving the instructions, and with Red in the saddle, Seabiscuit was schooled each morning to break him of his bad habits at the starting gate, then he was given a short workout on the track. The workouts were intended only to keep his muscles flexible and strong until he had regained his strength, but after a few mornings Seabiscuit wanted to turn on the speed, showing that he liked to run for the sheer joy of it. He no longer resented control or urging, and would answer a touch of Red's heel or whip with everything he had. With each day it became more noticeable that he was rapidly recovering from his exhaustion. He went at his oats as eagerly as he went at his workouts, and his lame knee had responded amazingly to Tom's brace-and-bandage treatment.

Although Seabiscuit had far from regained his full strength, he showed so much zest for all-out running that, after a week's training, Tom thought it best to enter him in a race. He had no great expectation of winning it, but was anxious to see how Seabiscuit would behave in competition now that his manners were improved. The race was the Motor City Handicap, run at the Fair Grounds track in Detroit on

August 22, at a mile and a sixteenth.

Showing marked improvement in his behavior at the starting gate, Seabiscuit got away in third position. He was still third at the quarter-mile post, and moved up to the lead by the time he had reached the half. Then, following Tom's instructions, Red slowed him until he was seventh when they rounded the end of the track and came into the homestretch. With straight going ahead, and little danger of putting ex cessive stress on the colt's weakened knee, Red let him run as he pleased from the head of the stretch — and he pleased to try his best. Although he still lacked the strength with which to put on a driving finish, he was fourth to go under the wire.

ROBERT RIGER

After ten days of rest, doctoring, dieting, and careful training, Seabiscuit was entered in another race at slightly over a mile. By that time he had gained enough strength, and his knee was sufficiently healed that Tom told Red to let the colt out all the way. Again Seabiscuit got away from the post in third position, pulled into the lead before the quarter was reached, and held it until the far turn from the backstretch. But he had not yet learned to answer the reins with absolute precision. He was running too wide at the end of the backstretch, was crowded out on the turn, and forced back into fourth position. There he was blocked by the horses in front of him until the turn into the homestretch was made, but he wouldn't give up, and came on to go under the wire half a length behind the winner.

That race left no doubt in the minds of owner, trainer, or jockey that Seabiscuit was ready and eager for top-notch competition. On September 7, he was entered in the Governor's Handicap, the most important race of the year at Detroit. He drew a bad post position — twelfth from the rail — and no one except the three men who knew and loved him thought he had the slightest chance of being in the money.

From his bad post position, Seabiscuit did well to get into fifth place at the quarter pole, and from there on he had to fight for every inch. At the half, he was third, gained second place in the backstretch, and held doggedly to it around the far end of the track. The moment he turned into the homestretch, he changed leads to favor his weak knee, then drove with all his might and courage. He came under the wire still driving, and winner by a neck. His share of the purse was $4290 — more than half of what Charles Howard had paid for him three weeks earlier.

Before leaving Detroit at the end of the month, Seabiscuit had paid back another $2010 of his cost; winning the Hendrie Handicap by four lengths. Added to this, the parimutuels had paid $11.80 for every two dollars bet on him — and the three men who knew him best believed in putting their money where they had put their confidence. With Tom and Red the amount of their wagers had been woefully small, but it doesn't take much at eleven-eighty to two.

After his double triumph at Detroit, Seabiscuit was shipped to the River Downs track at Cincinnati, where Mr. Howard had gathered a stable of eleven other Thoroughbreds. Among them was Exhibit, an extremely fast sprinter. To sharpen both horses for stretch drives, Tom decided to give Seabiscuit and Exhibit a few workouts together. It didn't work out. On their first run, they got away from the starting gate on the fly, then raced for an eighth of a mile shoulder-to-shoulder. Everyone had expected Exhibit, a sprinter, to run away from Seabiscuit, a distance runner, but Seabiscuit was determined not to be beaten. When he found himself hard pressed, he looked Exhibit squarely in the eye and snorted his challenge.

That was enough for the sprinter. He flung up his tail, dropped back, and refused to be worked again with his evil-eyed stablemate.

At Cincinnati Seabiscuit was run in two small handicap races during October; once on a dry track, and once in mud. By that time Mr. Howard had decided to enter him in the $5000-added Scarsdale Handicap at the Empire City track in New York, so the Cincinnati races were used as warm-ups. Red Pollard held the anxious colt in until the homestretch was reached, then let him make his run for the wire. In both races Seabiscuit made a fine stretch run, and finished third without being pushed.

It was barely more than two months from the time Seabiscuit left New York as an outcast until he was brought back to run in one of the richest races of the fall season. There the railbirds were still laughing about the old ex-cowboy who had no better sense than to think he could improve a colt that Sunny Jim Fitzsimmons had given up on. Their ridicule became raucous when they discovered that Seabiscuit would be ridden in the big race by Red Pollard, a bush-league jockey who had done most of his riding at western frontier shows. To them, any racing meet held west of the Hudson River — with the possible exception of Chicago — was bush-league, so they were entirely unimpressed by the colt's two wins at Detroit.

Charles Howard also came in for his share of ridicule by the railbirds. Who was he? Oh, some California automobile tycoon, with more money than good sense. Didn't know a race horse from a Jersey heifer! That Seabiscuit colt wasn't the only no-account nag he'd been stuck with; he'd picked up more than a dozen others. Not one in the bunch worth stall room and oats. Oh sure, that sort of a string might get by out in California where there weren't any decent horses and nobody knew anything about training, but this Howard guy must be out of his head to think he could make any kind of a showing at Empire City. The nerve of him! Entering a gimpy, broken-down dog like that son of Hard Tack in the Scarsdale Handicap! He might better pour his money down a rat hole than waste it on the entry fee.

The railbirds are the professional gamblers and track followers who get out to the track at the crack of dawn to watch and time the morning workouts. Their ridiculing couldn't help but reach Tom Smith's ears, but Silent Tom said nothing — and the more the railbirds talked the better he liked it. That kind of ridicule would drive the odds up in the parimutuel betting, and he and Red had nice little nest eggs from Seabiscuit's wins at Detroit. They had a friend who was going to put every nickel of their cash on the colt's nose in the Scarsdale Handicap, and the higher the odds the better.

Seabiscuit had never been so eager to turn on full speed, and he was rounding into hard, razor-sharp condition. Early each morning Tom and Red gave him an easy exercising on the training track, while the railbirds watched with their thumbs on the stems of their stopwatches. Then, in the afternoon when the birds had all flown away to watch the races, they sharpened the dark bay colt's speed and racing instinct to a slashing edge.

Possibly the greatest change that had taken place in Seabiscuit during the two months he had been with Tom Smith and Red Pollard was that he had found contentment. He never showed it more clearly than when he went to the starting gate for the Scarsdale Handicap. The last time the New York racing fans had seen him he had been fractious and unruly on his way to the post. In the Scarsdale he followed Pumpkin past the jam-packed grandstand with as much unconcern as if he were being led to pasture. Halfway past, he turned his head toward the stand, and looked the crowd over as though he wondered

what all the excitement was about. That did it! It was evident to the professional gamblers that he had no interest in racing, and by post time the odds against him had risen to twelve-to-one.

Seabiscuit had drawn the number-two position at the post. He walked calmly into his stall in the starting gate, and stood quietly while assistant starters coaxed the nervous, high-strung favorites into their places. Anyone watching the stubby-legged, slender colt might have thought him to be completely unconcerned, but Red Pollard could feel the muscles tense along his back as he stood poised and waiting for the starter's gong.

At the sound of the bell, Seabiscuit was away as though he had been shot from a catapult. In a dozen powerful strides, he reached the rail, and streaked past the grandstand out in front of the pack. He was still out in front at the quarter post, but Red drew him back into seventh place before the half was reached. The race was at a mile and seventy yards, and Tom had instructed him to save the colt's strength for a sprint in the homestretch.

In the backstretch, Red held Seabiscuit in eighth place, with the favorites, Emileo and Sergeant Byrne, well out in front. The race had been rough from the beginning, and at the far turn the leaders jammed together, each jockey fighting to gain an advantage in rounding the end of the track and coming into the homestretch. The moment the leaders began to bunch,

Red called on Seabiscuit to make his bid, pointing him toward the only opening where he might get through the jam. And Seabiscuit answered with everything he had. He shot through the narrow opening like water from a floodgate, but the front-runners were bunched tightly against the rail, so Red had to take him wide around the turn.

Coming into the homestretch, Seabiscuit was within four lengths of the leader, but well to the outside, and there were still five of the best three-year-olds in the East ahead of him. Red Pollard crouched low above the bay colt's withers, reached back, and slapped him once across the rump with his whip. Again Seabiscuit answered, but this time with that hidden reserve of power that only a champion can call upon in a crisis. And for Seabiscuit this was a crisis. He seemed to sense that he, his owner, his trainer, and his jockey had all been ridiculed, and that it was up to him to vindicate them. Ears tight to his neck, head low, and muzzle stretched out to the limit, he made his challenge.

No race is so exciting to the fans as one in which half a dozen outsiders have passed the favorites on the turn and are bunched in a homestretch battle for a big purse. The 1936 running of the Scarsdale Handicap was made to order for them. Both favorites had fallen back in the jamming at the far turn, and the five leaders in front of Seabiscuit were fighting it out neck-and-neck for the finish wire. The crowd, the largest of the fall season at Empire City, leaped to its feet and screamed like maniacs. But few, if any, besides Mr. and Mrs. Charles S. Howard, were cheering for the outcast son of Hard Tack. Four lengths back at the head of the stretch, and far to the outside, he had been completely lost sight of by the fans as they cheered on the front-runners. But they were helping to win Seabiscuit's race for him.

Man o' War was a showman of the highest order, and he had passed his showmanship on through his disgraceful son, Hard Tack. If ever a Thoroughbred race horse was a "ham," Seabiscuit was the one. He'd been parading his contentment and assurance to the fans when he passed the grandstand on his way to the post. He'd paraded his speed to them when he led the pack past the stands at the start. And now their cheers were a stimulant that sent the blood pounding through his great heart, and the indomitable will to win surging through his mind and muscles. Red Pollard had no need to touch him again with the whip — not with the sound of that crowd's cheering in his ears. Driving as he had never driven before, Seabiscuit caught up to the leaders a few lengths from the wire, snorted his challenge, and drove on to win by a nose. At the last moment, his ears pricked forward — a signal to the fans in the grandstand that he was still far from spent.

The $5570 purse Seabiscuit won in the Scarsdale Handicap didn't make Mr. and Mrs. Howard much wealthier than they already were. Their greatest re-

that their judgment of the outcast colt, and
fidence in him, had been more than vindi-
he had not only beaten every horse against
. . . . . , but every horse that had raced that distance at
Empire City. His time of one minute and forty-four
seconds had set a new track record. For Tom Smith
and Red Pollard, Seabiscuit had not only won fame,
but independence, for with the pari-mutuel odds at
twelve-to-one, their hard times were definitely ended.

When Seabiscuit stunned the New Yorkers by his
brilliant winning of the Scarsdale Handicap, the California winter racing season was just getting under way.
It is hardly surprising that Mr. and Mrs. Howard were
anxious to take their sensational colt there and let their
home-town friends see him in action. San Francisco
had two of the finest racing plants in the West — Tanforan, originally built in 1899; and the magnificent
Bay Meadows plant, built in 1934. As soon as the
meet at Empire City closed, Mr. Howard charted a
special car on the crack Overland Limited train, and
shipped his horses to Tanforan.

Thoroughbreds are now moved from track to track
in specially built horse vans that travel over smooth
highways, and if the trip requires more than a few
hours, the horses are unloaded for rest and exercise.
If the trip is a long one they are flown in horse trans-
port planes, and the flight time from coast to coast is
only a few hours. In 1936 it was quite a different
matter. Even on a crack passenger train such as the

Overland Limited, the journey from New York to San Francisco required four days and nights, with no stops for rest and exercise. Thoroughbreds, particularly race horses in training, are generally high-strung and nervous, making them notoriously poor railroad travelers. The long confinement, the constant clacking of the wheels, the swaying and the jolting, usually keep them from sleeping, throw them off their feed, upset their nerves, and stiffen their running muscles.

On the long journey from New York to San Francisco, Seabiscuit proved himself to be an excellent traveler. So long as he had Pumpkin for a stall mate, he was perfectly contented, ate like a boy scout on a camping trip, and slept like a baby. And Tom Smith watched over him as carefully as any mother could nurse her child. He slept within a few feet of Seabiscuit's stall, kept the braces on his knees to save them any possible strain, and kept his legs heavily padded with cotton and bandaged to protect them against bruises. But the braces and bandages were removed several times a day, and the legs and joints rubbed with liniment to keep them from stiffening.

The San Francisco racing fans and sports writers were as enthusiastic about Seabiscuit as the New Yorkers had been skeptical. When the Overland Limited pulled in and the Howard private car was shunted onto the sidetrack at Tanforan, an eager crowd was waiting to welcome the outcast colt that had humbled the best three-year-olds at Empire City. But

if they were excited by the arrival, Seabiscuit wasn't. Halfway down the ramp from the car, he stopped for a moment — just as any tourist might who was visiting California for the first time — and looked the place and the people over. Then he sauntered away to his barn with Tom Smith and Pumpkin, as unconcerned as a man going to his club for lunch.

The Tanforan season was nearly ended when the Howard horses arrived, but the big race of the meet — the $5000-added San Francisco Handicap — was to be run on the coming Saturday. Mr. and Mrs. Howard had planned that it would be Seabiscuit's California debut, for they were as anxious to show off their prize colt as the fans were to see him in action. But the weather turned rainy, and the track became heavy. Disappointing as it was to both the Howards and Tom Smith, they decided to scratch Seabiscuit from the race, even though they felt sure he could win it. His knees and ankles, although greatly strengthened and improved by Tom's care, could never fully recover from the abuse given them in the thirty-five races he had run as a two-year-old. To put him into hard competition on a heavy track might injure those weakened joints still further, and the risk couldn't be taken.

The Bay Meadows racing season opened immediately after the closing of Tanforan, the weather cleared, and both tracks dried into excellent condition. Because of the clamor of the fans, as well as their own impatience to let their friends see the colt in action, the Howards decided to enter Seabiscuit in the one-mile Bay Bridge Handicap, to be run at Bay Meadows on November 28.

With the Tanforan track closed and in good condition, Tom did his training of Seabiscuit there, rather than moving him a few miles farther down the Peninsula to Bay Meadows. He doubtlessly had two reasons for doing so; one of them being that he preferred to work alone — away from other trainers. The second was that railbirds are the same wherever Thoroughbreds are being raced, and that he knew how curious they would be about Seabiscuit's workouts. Even though Tanforan was closed and the other trainers had moved their horses to Bay Meadows, the railbirds were out with their stopwatches at the crack of dawn each morning. Tom did exactly as he had done at Empire City; exercised the colt a little each morning, then in the afternoon, when the stopwatch boys had gone to Bay Meadows for the races, he and Red let Seabiscuit run as fast as he liked.

Saturday, November 28, 1936, was a beautiful day at Bay Meadows, and a crowd of 12,000 was on hand to see the running of the Bay Bridge Handicap. Many of them were there for a first look at Seabiscuit, but he was far from being the favorite. The reports of sports writers and railbirds indicated that he hadn't yet recovered from his long trip across the country, and some of the fastest three-year-olds in the West were entered in the race. Uppermost, the favorite, had broken the track record only the week before, and Velociter had turned in some amazingly fast time in his workouts.

As in the Scarsdale Handicap, Seabiscuit strolled nonchalantly to the post, turning his head to look the crowd over as he passed the grandstand, then stood quietly in the starting gate as he waited for the sound of the gong. But the instant it rang his powerful hind legs struck out like twin battering rams. The thrust was so terrific that the ground broke from under his hoofs, throwing him off stride, and nearly to his knees. Before he could gather himself and regain his stride, the pack was well on its way to the clubhouse turn. Red had no choice but to drop into eighth place, bring Seabiscuit to the rail, and hold him there throughout the turn in order to save ground.

On turning into the backstretch, Red tried to move Seabiscuit up, but found himself caught behind a flying wedge of horses, with little chance to get out. There is an old axiom among race-horse men that there is only one sprint in a horse during each race; that if he is driven at top speed in the early part of a race at a mile or more, he will have nothing left with which to make a stretch drive. Red Pollard was faced with a situation where he had to risk spending Seabiscuit's sprint in order to get out from behind the wedge. He dropped low on the colt's withers, pointed him for the only possible opening, and touched him with his heels. If he had been driving a high-powered racing car, and tramped down on the gas pedal, the response couldn't have been more instantaneous. With an electrifying burst of speed, Seabiscuit shot through the narrow hole and began cutting down the gap between himself and the favorites. Velociter was nearing the far turn, with Uppermost tight behind, her jockey waiting to make his bid as the end of the track was being turned.

Again Red found himself blocked. His only hope was to call for another all-out burst of speed, pull to the outside, and turn the end of the track wide enough that it would lengthen the distance to the wire by at least a length. Seabiscuit answered the second call with fully as much speed as the first. He had passed Uppermost, and was pulling alongside Velociter at the center of the turn. To drive him still wider and out of the race, Velociter's jockey bore out, letting Uppermost slip through on the rail and take the lead for a moment. But it was for only a moment. Seabiscuit laid his ears back, snorted his challenge at both favorites, then surged ahead and led the way into the homestretch by a full length.

The race was over. Neither of the favorites had the courage to withstand such a whirlwind challenge. They dropped back and let Sunny Jim's outcast canter under the wire five lengths in the lead — setting a new track record for Bay Meadows, and adding $1970 to his winnings.

The San Francisco fans and sports writers went wild

with joy, and headlines were splashed across all the big newspapers of the state. Californians, newcomers to big-time horse racing, had been yearning for a colt that might bring a championship to their state, and many of them thought they had found one. In the *San Francisco News,* Tom Laird wrote, "He isn't much to look at as horses go, and he might easily be passed up for a more flashy looking horse in the Howard barn, but when he's under colors and turns on that sensational burst of speed, which he seems capable of turning on at any stage of the race, there's no mistaking his ability. He has what it takes in a surplus quantity."

The biggest race of the Bay Meadows season was the $10,000 World's Fair Handicap, at a mile and three-sixteenths, run on December 12. For Seabiscuit, this was just another race — another chance to show what he could do for men who understood and loved him. At the first turn he took the lead, never gave it up, and romped home, winner by five lengths, to set another track record and bring his winnings for the four months he had been in the Howard stable to $23,030 — nearly three times the value Sunny Jim Fitzsimmons had placed on him.

Again the California fans went wild with enthusiasm, and were sure they had found a champion, but no man who knew horse racing could believe it to be any more than wishful hoping. No horse that had been as abused as Seabiscuit, when a two-year-old, had ever amounted to much afterwards. And even if he

hadn't been mistreated and overworked, his chances of greatness were, beyond any doubt, past. No race horse had ever become a champion without being close to the top as a three-year-old, for most of the big purses were for that age. From then on a horse was handicapped by being required to carry additional weight to offset his speed, and only a superhorse could win consistently under such conditions.

Amazing as the latter part of Seabiscuit's season had been, he was a long, long way from being the top three-year-old of 1936. That honor, as well as being top money winner of the year for all ages, had gone to his pampered rival, Granville. He had won only seven races, while Seabiscuit had won nine, but had been entered in only high-purse races, and had won $110, 295 — more money than it seemed possible for the outcast to win in his entire lifetime. When, on January 1, 1937, both colts became four-year-olds, no one could have said that Sunny Jim Fitzsimmons hadn't shown good judgment in favoring Granville over Seabiscuit right from the start.

4

Since early colonial times horse racing has been one of the most popular sports in America. By 1650 quarter-mile races were being run on paths cut through the woods near the larger settlements of Virginia and Maryland. Then, following the Revolutionary War, Thoroughbreds were imported from England, race tracks were built near our larger cities, and the horsemen of this country went painstakingly about establishing and improving royal American Thoroughbred families. Their efforts were rewarded when, nearly a century and a half later, Man o' War set five world speed records in the eleven races he ran as a three-year-old.

Ever since the time of the Roman Empire, men have

taken tremendous pride in the speed of their fast horses, have raced them against each other, and have wagered on the outcome of the races. The demand for exceptionally fast racers became so great, and their cost so high, that only the nobility could afford to own them, so horse racing became known as "The Sport of Kings."

Originally, most of the wagering was done between these wealthy owners, but as the sport became popular the common people began flocking to the races, choosing favorites, and betting with each other on the outcome. As a result, the races were held on courses near large centers of population, admission was charged, and part of the money received was offered as prizes to the owners of the winning horses. The greater the crowd, the higher the prizes, so the fastest horses were usually raced near the largest cities.

When this country won its independence and our government was formed, each state was empowered to pass laws for the regulation of activities within its borders. By that time horse racing had become the most popular sport in the new nation, and wherever horses were raced the fans thronged to the courses and bet on their favorites. But the churches were opposed to gambling. They were successful in having anti-wagering laws passed in New England, and in many of the new states established in the West. Until the anti-wagering laws were repealed, there was little or no horse racing in these states, for large crowds would attend the races only if they could bet on the outcome. But in New York, Pennsylvania, and the South, racing flourished, and there the American Thoroughbred was developed into the fastest horse on earth.

As the population of our cities grew, New York became the horse-racing capital of the United States. Other cities along the Atlantic Coast, and inland as far as the Mississippi River, became lesser centers, but there was almost no Thoroughbred racing in the West.

When, in 1933, pari-mutuel wagering on horse races was legalized in California, Los Angeles sportsmen went all-out to make their city one of the racing capitals of the world. In order to do it, they built multi-million-dollar Santa Anita Park — the most luxurious horse-racing plant in the United States. But that was not enough. The great racing stables, with their top-notch Thoroughbreds, were all in the East. If Los Angeles were to become a racing capital, the finest horses in the land must be brought there to race, and owners would risk shipping their most valuable horses across the entire country only if the prizes to be won were well worth the risks. To entice the big owners in the East to ship their finest racers to Los Angeles, Charles H. Strub, general manager of Santa Anita Park, inaugurated the $100,000 Santa Anita Handicap — the richest horse-racing stake ever to have been offered in the world.

Building Santa Anita Park and bringing there the richest horse-racing event in the world was an ambitious undertaking. But the fondest ambition of the California sportsmen was to develop a horse capable of winning the great event against the fastest Thoroughbreds the East could produce. They expected the task to take many years, for it had required more than a century to establish the royal Thoroughbred families in the East, and the wealthy owners there would not give up a colt that showed promise of becoming a champion.

The first glimmer of hope came for the Californians when Seabiscuit won the Scarsdale Handicap at Empire City, and then came West to set two successive track records at Bay Meadows. The leading California bookmaker immediately named him as favorite in the Santa Anita Handicap, to be run at the end of February, much to the ridicule of the railbirds in the East. They compared his record to Granville's, and scoffed at his Bay Meadows records, saying that either the miles were shorter in California than in New York or the stopwatches were slower.

It is doubtful that the California bookmaker actually believed Seabiscuit capable of winning the Santa Anita Handicap, but there was no doubt of it in the minds of Charles Howard, Tom Smith, or Red Pollard. Beyond that, Mr. Howard was one of the sportsmen who had financed Santa Anita Park, and his fondest hope was to bring California the honor of producing a horse that could win its richest racing prize.

Seabiscuit was shipped to Santa Anita in the middle of December, where it was planned to give him a few weeks' rest, with just enough training to bring him into tiptop condition for the $100,000 handicap. But Ollie Olson nearly upset the plans.

Soon after Seabiscuit was brought to California, Ollie had been hired as the colt's private groom. And, like all of the little outcast's "own-folks," Ollie fell head-over-heels in love with him. Under Tom Smith's coaching, he learned to massage the weakened joints and tendons, to put on the knee braces, and to use exactly the right amount of liniment before bandaging the colt's legs with thick paddings of cotton. Each day Tom weighed out the menu for the colt: so much cold bran mash for breakfast, so many pints of oats for dinner and supper, and exactly so many pounds of oat-and-timothy hay.

Ollie slept in Seabiscuit's stall, called him Baby, as Red Pollard did, and followed Tom Smith's instructions exactly in all but one way. He, like Seabiscuit, was a hearty eater, and it broke his heart to see Baby being starved. Each night, when Tom and Red were safely in bed and asleep, Ollie would sneak a generous hot bran mash into the stall, just as a before-bedtime snack for Baby. Then, during the day, he smuggled in a few pints of oats in his pockets. And each pint went into speed-reducing fat on the colt's ribs.

By the time Tom discovered what was going on, Seabiscuit was beginning to look like a prize beef steer, and no safe amount of exercise would keep him down to his best racing weight. But Tom found himself in a dilemma. Even under threats of firing, Ollie wouldn't stop his smuggling, and Tom didn't dare fire him anyway. Seabiscuit had become so attached to his generous groom that he became very nervous and irritable when Ollie was not in his stall at night. At last Tom had to appeal to Mrs. Howard, for Ollie worshiped her and would do whatever she told him — even to starving Baby.

For a couple of weeks Tom Smith and Red Pollard had to exercise the colt briskly both morning and afternoon before they could strip him of his extra fat and round him again into racing condition. As always the railbirds were on hand to watch the early morning workouts and to check the speed on their stopwatches. But Tom Smith, as he had done at other tracks, gave them little speed to check, while other trainers put their horses through a few fast workouts. The horses that showed the best time on the stopwatches were Rosemont and Time Supply, two of the best handicap horses from the East, so the railbirds made them favorites over Seabiscuit for the big race.

When sharpening Thoroughbreds for a very important race, most trainers like to start them in a couple of lesser races, a week or two in advance, so warm-up races are usually scheduled on the racing program. At Santa Anita, the warm-up events were the Huntington Beach Handicap, run on February

9, and the San Antonio Handicap, run on February 20. Most of the horses that would start in the big race were entered, and Rosemont was made the favorite at odds of five-to-one, while Time Supply and Seabiscuit were ten-to-one.

From the start of the Huntington Beach Handicap it was evident the three favorites had not yet reached the peak of their racing form, but Seabiscuit was bubbling over with eagerness to run. He broke from his number five post position in full stride, caught the fast-sprinting leader, Cloud D'Or, before reaching the quarter post, and appeared to be tantalizing him through the backstretch — keeping barely a neck in front, but running effortlessly. Coming into the home-stretch, Seabiscuit was a half-length ahead. Then, without the slightest urging from Red Pollard, he turned on a blinding burst of speed, as if taunting the railbirds who had driven the betting odds against him to twice those against Rosemont. At the finish line his ears were up and he was coasting — six full lengths ahead of Time Supply, with Rosemont another four lengths farther back.

The San Antonio Handicap was the final rehearsal for the great $100,000 Santa Anita classic, and sixteen horses were entered. Because of his easy victory in the Huntington Beach, Seabiscuit was made the favorite at odds of five-to-two, but finished fifth, four lengths behind Rosemont, the winner. He had drawn number eleven post position, was badly interfered with at the start, and in twelfth place before he could reach the rail. He was still twelfth at the three-quarter pole, and blocked off by the tightly bunched horses in front of him. On the far turn, Red had to swing him very wide to get past, and they came into the home-stretch eight and a half lengths behind Rosemont. There was no possible chance of winning, but again Seabiscuit put on an electrifying stretch run, gaining four and a half lengths on Rosemont in the final fur-long. Great as his race had been, his finishing out of the money was enough to drop him to third place among the favorites for the big race.

February 27, 1937, was a warm, sunny day in South-ern California. The track was in perfect condition for the Santa Anita Handicap — and so was Seabiscuit. Tom Smith had trained off every ounce of his fat, brought him to a hard, tough fitness, and honed his rac-ing instinct to rapier sharpness. Mr. Howard, Tom, and Red Pollard hadn't the slightest doubt that he would win, and had laid their plans for the race care-fully. Through the early part of the race and the backstretch, Seabiscuit was to be held just behind the leaders, then brought to the front while rounding the turn, so there would be no danger of his being blocked while making his powerful drive down the home-stretch.

When, a few minutes after four o'clock, eighteen of the fastest Thoroughbreds in the world paraded to the post, more than sixty thousand fans jammed the grandstand and overflowed into the infield. Among them were the railbirds — drawn as by a magnet from every part of the country — doctors, lawyers, bootblacks, tourists, almost the entire Hollywood movie colony, and countless Californians who had trekked to Santa Anita in the hope of seeing Seabiscuit, their Cinderella horse, win the great racing classic.

Beyond the finish line, the clubhouse and private boxes glittered with the elite of society and the racing world; the press box was crowded with sports writers from every big newspaper in the United States, and more than a million and a half dollars had already passed through the betting windows.

With the race at a mile and a quarter, and the oval only a mile around, the start was from a straightaway chute, a furlong beyond the farthest end of the grandstand. As the horses lined up in the gate — tall, handsome Rosemont near the outside, and little Seabiscuit third from the rail — the huge throng stood in hushed silence, anxiously awaiting the running of the richest racing event in the world. Then, to the deafening roar of *"THEY'RE OFF,"* a wall of Thoroughbreds broke from the gate like a swirling flood from a broken dam. From the grandstand and clubhouse the shouting crowd could see little more than a seething mass of horses, rushing toward it down the chute like a mighty torrent on a rampage. And above the surging river of horses, the jockeys in their bright silks tossed like cockleshells riding the crest of a flood.

Seabiscuit was ninth away from the barrier. Through the turmoil of the first furlong Red Pollard maneuvered him deftly, avoiding interference, shooting him through any opening that appeared, and jockeying for position. As the leaders strung out and swept for the first time past the cheering crowd in the grandstand, Red brought Seabiscuit easily into fourth place, then held him there past the clubhouse and into the first turn. Well out in the lead, the speedster, Special Agent, set a scorching early pace. Behind him streaked Boxthorn, one of the most highly regarded stake horses in the country, closely followed by gigantic Don Roberto. Far back, Harry Richards, the top stakewinning jockey of 1936, had gone to the whip, trying to bring Rosemont into contention from his poor starting position.

Around the turn and up the backstretch, the four leaders held their positions like horses on a merry-go-round. Going into the far turn, Red hunched low over Seabiscuit's withers, touched him with his heels, and called on him to make his bid. He answered with a surge of speed that neither Don Roberto nor Boxthorn could match, passed them at the top of the turn, and bore down on the tiring Special Agent. As the Californians roared themselves hoarse in cheering on their Cinderella horse, he winged past Special Agent on the outside, turned into the homestretch leading by a head, gained the rail, and opened his lead to a full length.

At the paddock runway Tom Smith took the straw he'd been chewing from his mouth, and in the clubhouse Mr. and Mrs. Howard glowed with pride and happiness. The race had gone exactly as they'd planned it, and with Seabiscuit a length out in front, they couldn't believe that any horse living had the slightest chance of catching him before he reached the wire.

Unfortunately, Red Pollard had the same belief, and let Seabiscuit hug close to the rail, where the track was softest and slowest. But Harry Richards hadn't become top stake-winning jockey without learning all the tricks of the trade. Through the backstretch and around the turn, he had done the most skillful job of riding ever seen at Santa Anita; threading Rosemont through any opening that showed, going to the whip when needed, but holding back enough of his mount's energy for a driving finish. Rounding into the near turn he slipped past Don Roberto and Boxthorn, swept wide into the homestretch and overhauled Special Agent.

Keeping well out from the rail, where the track was hard and fast, Richards drove for the wire with his whip slashing, and under the punishment long-legged Rosemont ran as he had never run before. While the fans in the grandstand and the celebrities in the clubhouse went frantic with excitement, he shortened the gap between himself and short-legged Seabiscuit by a foot or more at every leap.

The finish of the race was best described by Grantland Rice, the most famous sports writer of his day. In his article in the *Los Angeles Times,* he wrote, "In the last hundred yards Seabiscuit had the lead by half a length. But in that final swirl it was Richards who went to the whip as he practically lifted Rosemont across. For some reason Red Pollard left the whip in his scabbard, figuring he had the race in hand. But that final whiplash from Richards turned the $100,000 trick. It lifted Rosemont across the line by a foot or so, with Seabiscuit struggling desperately to hold the lead he had picked up through the finish." Other sports writers were less charitable, saying that Red had thrown the race away through lack of skill and judgment.

Most of us are inclined to claim full credit for our successes, but to blame others, or ill-fortune, for our failures and disappointments. The mark of sterling character in a man or woman is the ability to accept with understanding and kindness the disappointments and heartbreaks that have been caused by another's failures. Never in the history of horse racing has sterling character been more clearly demonstrated than in Seabiscuit's defeat in the Santa Anita Handicap of 1937.

We all have some fond ambition, some goal we would rather attain than any other in life. If the attainment is little more than an idle dream, completely beyond our reach, the pain of giving it up is small.

But to hold it in our grasp, then see it slip away at the last instant is heartbreaking. From the time Santa Anita Park was built, Mr. and Mrs. Howard's fondest hope had been to bring to their beloved California a winner for its own great racing classic. And ever since Tom Smith had patched up his first Thoroughbred, he had yearned to develop a winner for the richest racing prize in the world. To have their hopes so nearly realized, then shattered in the final stride of the great classic, was a sad disappointment, but not heartbreaking. Their heartbreak was for Seabiscuit, the knobby-kneed, gallant little outcast that had given them his very best, and through no fault of his own, had lost his one big chance to attain greatness.

There wasn't the slightest doubt in Mr. and Mrs. Howard's or Tom Smith's minds that Seabiscuit was the fastest and most courageous race horse in the world. But, though they wouldn't admit it even to themselves, they knew that his chance of attaining greatness was now less than one in a thousand. No colt so abused as he had been in his early racing career had ever held up for more than a couple of years. Regardless of what care was given him, the injury to his leg joints and tendons could never be fully healed, and it was just a matter of time before they would break down under the terrific strain of racing. If he could have won the Santa Anita Handicap, with its $100,000 first prize, he might have been able to pass Granville's record for winnings in a single year. Without the big prize that had slipped away in the final stride, the task seemed entirely hopeless. It could be accomplished only by winning eight or more of the richest stakes open to horses above three years old. And that would be a task for a superhorse, not a little one with weak knees, for consistent stake winners are handicapped by being required to carry tremendous loads.

Heartbroken as Mr. and Mrs. Howard and Tom Smith were at Seabiscuit's having lost his bid for greatness, their grief was small compared to Red Pollard's. Ever since the day he had first leaned on the colt's stall door, the affection between them had grown, and their confidence in each other had strengthened. Red needed no one to tell him that he had let that affection and confidence lose the race, that a few clips of the whip through the homestretch would have sent Baby under the wire an easy winner.

Many a jockey has been dropped by a racing stable, or berated by owner and trainer for losing a race that he should have won, but neither Mr. and Mrs. Howard nor Tom Smith had a word of criticism for Red Pollard. They had only compassion for his grief, acknowledged that their own overconfidence had been as much to blame for the loss as his, and defended him stoutly against the critics who tried to belittle his skill or judgment. Although they knew there was barely more than a hope that Seabiscuit's knees and tendons could hold up that long, they told Red, "Forget about this race. We were all in it together, and lost it because we were too sure 'of ourselves, but we know we have the best horse in the world. We'll win many another race before this year is over, and next year we'll come back and win the big one."

The last important event of the Santa Anita season was the $10,000 San Juan Capistrano Handicap to be run on the Saturday following the big race. Though the prize for the winner was only a tenth as much, the interest of the fans was nearly as great, for the race was at a mile and an eighth, and Indian Broom, the world's record holder at that distance, had been nominated, together with his speed-burning stablemate, Special Agent.

The ideal race would be one in which all the horses were exactly matched in speed and endurance. But this is impossible, for a horse's speed will vary with the fineness of the edge to which he has been trained, the amount of rest he has had between races, the condition of the track, the distance to be run, and numerous other factors. In order to equalize the speed of all horses in a race as much as possible, a system of handicapping has been devised. It is based on the knowledge that a horse's speed is slowed about two lengths to the mile for every additional pound of weight he is required to carry. Every track has a Racing Secretary or professional handicapper who studies the recent performances of each horse nominated for a race, then assigns the additional weight, if any, that each shall carry. And to bring the weight of jockey, saddle, and pad up to the requirements, lead plates are inserted in the saddle pad.

In the Santa Anita Handicap, Seabiscuit, carrying 115 pounds, had barely caught Special Agent at a mile and an eighth. And Indian Broom, carrying 116 pounds, had moved up to take third place, a length and a half behind Rosemont. On the theory that an extra pound of weight slows a horse two lengths to the mile, Indian Broom, the world's record holder, should have beaten Seabiscuit by more than half a length if they had been carrying equal weight. But in setting the weights for the San Juan Capistrano Handicap, Seabiscuit was required to carry 120 pounds, Indian Broom only 118, and Special Agent 116.

When the handicap weights for the San Juan Capistrano race were announced, Mr. Howard had felt them to be unfair. He was reluctant to enter Seabiscuit, and did so only because of the clamor of the fans and the urging of Tom Smith. Tom knew how anxious Red was to redeem his loss in the big race, and he knew that Seabiscuit would have no trouble in carrying the 120-pound load. In their late afternoon sessions, he and Red had been breezing the stouthearted four-year-old with loads as high as 125 pounds, and found him as eager and able as ever to turn on top speed. Their only regret was that Rosemont wouldn't be entered in the Capistrano.

Ten horses went to the post, but to the 45,000 fans who thronged the grandstand there were only three

that counted — Seabiscuit, Indian Broom, and Special Agent; the last two owned by the same stable. No fan watching that race could have failed to see that Red Pollard was out to prove Seabiscuit a better horse than Rosemont, even though the winner of the Santa Anita was not in the race. And no horseman could have failed to see that Seabiscuit was fully as determined as Red.

At the sound of the starter's bell, Red sent Seabiscuit quickly into the lead with a smack or two of his whip. Then Special Agent shot by them as though he were running a quarter-mile dash. Without the slightest urging, Seabiscuit answered the challenge in a sizzling burst of speed. Matching stride for stride, they sped past the howling crowd in the grandstand a half-dozen lengths in front of the pack, then flew into the first turn like frightened antelopes. There Red sat back on the reins, pulling the overeager Seabiscuit to a reasonable pace. It was clear to him that they were being caught in a trap. Special Agent was being used as a decoy to steal the race for Indian Broom. His jockey had obviously been instructed to set a pace fast enough to run Seabiscuit into exhaustion during the first mile, then Indian Broom would be brought up to win in a homestretch sprint.

All through the backstretch Red held Seabiscuit a length or two behind Special Agent, then turned him loose to make his bid. In a score of tremendous leaps, he caught the tiring front-runner at the top of the turn, then ran shoulder to shoulder with him into the homestretch.

Scientists tell us that a horse has no reasoning ability; that all his actions are governed by instinct and training. Even so, a highly intelligent horse has the ability to sense a situation with such keenness that it is closely akin to reasoning, and few Thoroughbreds ever matched Seabiscuit for intelligence. There was never a finer demonstration of it than in the finish of the San Juan Capistrano Handicap. One might almost have believed he had been reading the sports pages, knew the criticism that had been heaped upon his friend Red Pollard, and was determined to avenge it. Beyond that, he appeared to thoroughly understand the trap that had been set by the trainer of Special Agent and Indian Broom, and to be ridiculing him for trying any such foolishness.

In running shoulder to shoulder with Special Agent, Seabiscuit was little more than coasting, for his ears were up, and he never once snorted his usual challenge. As they rounded the turn into the homestretch, Indian Broom's jockey went to the whip, bringing the world's record holder up fast to steal the race in the final furlong. But something went wrong. Seabiscuit appeared to have been lying back and waiting for that move. With no urging from Red, but with a burst of speed that neither Indian Broom, Rosemont, nor any other living horse could have matched, he streaked for the finish wire. It was as though he were showing the critics what he couldn't tell them; that Red had not been at fault in failing to use the whip in the big race — that the fault had been his own overconfidence.

With Red Pollard standing in the stirrups, holding him back with his full weight — and with the frenzied crowd roaring, "Bring on Rosemont! Bring on Rosemont!" — Seabiscuit hurled his 120-pound load across the finish line to break the track record by four-fifths of a second. Special Agent and Indian Broom, with their lighter loads, trailed eight lengths behind, so exhausted that they were being passed by Grand Manitou, a rank outsider.

There was no doubt in anyone's mind that Seabiscuit — in one minute, forty-eight and two-fifths seconds — had more than redeemed himself, his owners, his trainer, and his jockey. The sports writers who had been most critical the week before were now the loudest in their praises: "Jockey Jack Pollard, whose slightly overconfident finish on Seabiscuit lost the big race to Rosemont last Saturday, redeemed himself with one of the finest saddle exhibitions of the season."

"They're toasting a new champion today — Seabiscuit! The short-coupled little four-year-old son of Hard Tack and Swing On proved definitely superior to Rosemont by comparison as he handled his top weight of 120 pounds with ease, and dashed to a new track record."

"In a breath-taking performance which easily overshadowed Rosemont's triumph in the $100,000 stake, Seabiscuit thrilled 45,000 cheering racegoers as he crushed his rivals under a stinging defeat. He proved himself a real champion, and may rule the stakes division on the American turf this year. Certainly, he will run Rosemont dizzy if they ever hook up again.''

5

ONLY one thing could have made Mr. and Mrs. Howard, Tom Smith, and Red Pollard happier than to have the sports writers acknowledge Seabiscuit to be a real champion, superior to the horse that had nosed him out in the Santa Anita Handicap. And that one thing was to have had him win the classic itself, since, for a Thoroughbred, lasting greatness must be won on the tracks, not in newspaper columns. Between themselves they determined that everything humanly possible should be done to give Seabiscuit his chance to win the Santa Anita classic the following year. But no one knew better than they that it would require nothing short of magic to keep his weakened legs in condition for the task.

Fortunately, Mr. and Mrs. Howard had no interest in making money on horse racing. To them racing was a sport, a friendly rivalry between California and the big eastern owners for the honor of winning the richest prize in racing — the Santa Anita Handicap. Equally fortunate for Seabiscuit, Tom Smith's skill as a trainer was remarkably close to wizardry, and all Red Pollard needed to make him a top-flight jockey was experience. But more important than any of these was the affection and understanding that bound Tom, Red, the Howards, and Seabiscuit into an unbeatable combination.

Following the San Juan Capistrano Handicap, plans were carefully laid for bringing Seabiscuit through the 1937 season with the utmost care and preparing him, if possible, for a second chance at the Santa Anita Handicap. No expense was to be spared, and regardless of the money prizes that might be won, he would be raced only often enough to keep him in tiptop form. Even then, he would be entered only when a track was in perfect condition, when the handicap weight assigned him was reasonable, and when the honor to be won was great enough to justify the risk of injury.

The San Francisco spring racing season opened when the Los Angeles winter season closed. Mr. Howard and Tom decided to ship Seabiscuit there for a couple of the most important races at both the Tanforan and Bay Meadows tracks. Then, if he did well and showed no signs of injury, they planned to take him East for the summer campaign, where he could be raced against the finest stake horses in the country.

News of the drubbing Seabiscuit had given Indian Broom and Special Agent spread through racing circles of the country like wildfire, and San Francisco fans, claiming him for their own, went wild in their eagerness to see him in action again. On March 14, the Sunday newspapers blazed with headlines, *"Seabiscuit Here!"* And a leading sports writer began his column, "Seabiscuit, the horse with a hundred thousand friends, arrived at Tanforan siding yesterday in regal style. Charley Howard's mighty little horse occupied one entire end of a Pullman car, and immediately after being unloaded was taken to a special stall to await his engagements in the $5,000 Exposition and $10,000 Marchbank Handicaps."

At Tanforan the weather during the last half of March and the first week in April was beautiful, and Tom Smith took full advantage of it. Each morning at dawn, while the railbirds flocked to the track with stopwatches in hand, he and Red gave Seabiscuit a little loosening-up exercise. Then, late in the afternoon, they took him out again, to let him revel in the bursts of speed that were sheer joy to him, and that kept his running muscles tuned to the vibrancy of fiddle strings.

As April 10 drew nearer, it was hard to guess whether

Seabiscuit or the San Francisco fans were the most anxious for the running of the Exposition Handicap. Without a race for more than a month, Seabiscuit was so eager to run that Red could hardly hold him back in his morning exercise, and the fans were equally excited, for they had made the Cinderella horse their favorite over the best Thoroughbreds in the West. Then, at almost the last minute, Mr. Howard scratched his entry from the race. There was no doubt that Seabiscuit could have won it, but Tom Smith didn't want him to run. It had rained the night before, the track was heavy, the handicapper had assigned Seabiscuit top weight, and Tom was afraid the colt might injure himself trying to carry it in the heavy going.

In their disappointment at the scratching, the fans were loud in their criticism of Tom, and the railbirds spread the rumor that he was afraid of the competition, not the chance injury, pointing out that Seabiscuit's workouts had been far from impressive. But again the little bay four-year-old seemed to sense the criticism, and to feel that he should turn the tables on his friend's detractors.

The afternoon of April 17 was bright and sunny at Tanforan, the stands and clubhouse overflowed with the largest crowd of the season, and the track was in perfect condition. There were only two things that kept Tom Smith chewing at the end of a straw: Seabiscuit had been handicapped with top weight of

124 pounds, and had drawn the number seven post position. But if Tom was a bit worried, Seabiscuit wasn't. When Red rode him onto the track, he looked over the crowd in the grandstand as if he were deciding whether or not it was big enough to put on a show for. Then, as one of the sports writers put it, he followed the other fifteen starters to the post looking about as animated as Will Rogers going for a drink of water.

For the Marchbank Handicap, Seabiscuit stood relaxed in the starting gate, while the other contenders reared and danced in excitement. His whole attitude appeared to say, "Take it easy, boys. There won't be anything for you to do anyway. I came out to put on a solo act for my owners' home-town folks."

And that's just what he did. At the sound of the bell he shot from his stall as though he'd been stung by a wasp. From his number seven position, he gained the rail and took the lead in a dozen leaps. When, at an eighth of a mile, he made his first pass before the grandstand, he was so far out in front that the race looked like a pack of huntsmen chasing a stag. This time Red didn't pull him in at the first turn, but let him set his own pace. And how he did set it! By the end of the mile he had run the best horses in the West right off their feet. Then, his job taken care of, he coasted home with his 124-pound load, breaking another track record and exactly duplicating the time he had posted in the San Juan Capistrano Handicap.

After Seabiscuit's sparkling victory at Tanforan, Mr. and Mrs. Howard, as well as Tom Smith and Red Pollard, were determined that he should be given his chance to compete against the finest stake horses in the East. But to give him the chance would be risky, for he could meet the finest only if entered in eight or ten of the most grueling handicap races, where he would be required to carry heavy loads, and where the strain on his legs would be tremendous.

No human athlete was ever more carefully prepared for the Olympics than Tom Smith, Red Pollard, and Ollie Olson prepared Seabiscuit for his eastern campaign. Day after day and week after week he was put through exercises that Tom devised for strengthening the tendons of his weakened forelegs. And with each day the understanding between horse and rider became closer, until Baby would answer instantly the slightest touch of Red's hand or heel. When "Son," as Tom Smith called Seabiscuit, was in his stall Ollie was with him constantly, massaging, grooming, bandaging his legs half a dozen times a day with fresh liniment, and weighing every bite of grain and hay he ate.

No doctor could have taken greater care in prescribing the diet for an invalid than Tom Smith took in balancing and planning Seabiscuit's daily feedings. In his bush-league days he had discovered an exceptionally fine quality of timothy hay, grown in a little valley in northern California. He insisted that Son have no other timothy, and that it be mixed equally with oat hay, cut and cured when the full strength of the sap was in the foliage. For oats, the most important part of a race horse's feed, he demanded the finest white variety grown in the Sacramento Valley, and varied the amount at each feeding — enough to keep Seabiscuit's strength and vitality at the highest possible peak, but never enough to let him put on a pound of surplus fat. Even for stall bedding, Tom insisted on top-quality rice straw, free of dust, dirt or chaff.

During late April and early May there were several races at the Tanforan and Bay Meadows tracks that Seabiscuit could have won with little more effort than he used in his training workouts. His winnings in these races might have been several thousand dollars, but the honor to be won was small, so neither Mr. Howard nor Tom would agree to entering him, regardless of the insistence of the fans. The most important race remaining for the California spring season was the $10,000 Bay Meadows Handicap, to be run on May 22. For this race Tom prepared both Seabiscuit and his stablemate, Exhibit, but he put his greatest preparation on getting ready for the eastern campaign.

The Bay Meadows Handicap was little more than a solo performance for Seabiscuit. He so far outclassed the competition that the racing secretary handicapped him with twenty-two pounds more weight than Exhibit was required to carry. That should have slowed him by more than forty lengths in the mile-and-a-sixteenth race, but it wasn't enough. Seabiscuit trailed Exhibit through the backstretch and around the far turn, loafing along as if giving his stablemate the courtesy of being the front-runner. Then, at the head of the homestretch, he put on a little burst of speed, just enough to take him under the wire a length and a half in front. The time was not sensational — there was no need for it to be — and though the San Francisco fans went wild about their "Wonder horse," the eastern railbirds and handicappers were unimpressed.

The week after his victory in the Bay Meadows Handicap, Seabiscuit set off for his invasion of the East. He, his mascot Pumpkin, and Ollie Olson rode in a special Pullman car, followed by another that was loaded to the top with California hay, oats, and rice straw. Tom Smith was taking no chances on eastern hay, oats or moldy straw, for he was out to prove to the world what he, Red Pollard, and the Howards had known for six months: that Seabiscuit was the finest and fastest race horse in the world. Beyond that, Tom and Red were sick and tired of being twitted about Rosemont's having stolen the Santa Anita Handicap in the final stride, and Seabiscuit would again be meeting Rosemont in the $20,000 Brooklyn Handicap. Besides, he would be meeting Top Row, winner of the 1936 Santa Anita classic; Aneroid, the New Yorkers' choice as the best stake horse in America, and the finest handicap horses the East could muster.

Although the eastern railbirds were still belittling

Seabiscuit's victories in the West, the New York handicapper was only half skeptical. Believing Rosemont to be the best horse nominated for the Brooklyn Handicap, he weighted him with 127 pounds, but gave Seabiscuit and Aneroid 122, and let Top Row by with only 120 pounds to carry. The New York sports writers were completely skeptical. The morning of the race, one of them wrote in his column, "Rosemont, who has made a name for himself in the East, is taken as a horse with class. The Howard horse is thought of as a glorified plater in the Empire State, and today must really show his class to be rated in further races."

The next morning the same reporter was singing a different tune — and he had good reason for it. Seabiscuit and Aneroid had run away from Rosemont by half a city block. Never since the Brooklyn Handicap was inaugurated in 1887 had there been so exciting a finish, and never had a frenzied crowd of skeptics taken a horse to their hearts as they did Seabiscuit. While the fans nearly tore the stands down, he and Aneroid put on a homestretch battle that was unique in the history of New York Thoroughbred racing. From the head of the stretch they came bulldogging for the wire shoulder to shoulder — Seabiscuit, a bit off form from his five weeks of idleness and the long trip across the country, snorting his challenge at an adversary that wouldn't give up. But there was no giving up in Aneroid. He, too, was a descendant of the Fair Play – Ben Brush strain, and didn't know the meaning of

91

surrender. Two lengths from the wire Aneroid gained the lead by a neck, but neither Seabiscuit nor Red Pollard would be denied. At the last stride, Red called on him for his best, and he answered with a leap that took him under the wire, winner by a nose.

When Seabiscuit lost the Santa Anita Handicap, his chance of achieving greatness had seemed all but gone. The only possibilities remaining were that he might be kept in shape to come back and win the $100,000 classic in a second try, or that by some miracle his forelegs might hold up long enough to win a dozen or more of the rich handicap races in the East. After he finished the rugged Brooklyn Handicap sound and in excellent condition, Tom Smith had little fear of his breaking down, and the chances of his attaining greatness on the eastern tracks looked bright. His lion's share of the Brooklyn purse had brought his winnings for the year to $64,000, and three of the richest races of the eastern season were yet to be run — the Butler, Yonkers, and Massachusetts handicaps — each of them two weeks apart. It was decided to nominate him for all three, since, if he could win them, he would certainly become champion money-winning horse of the year, far surpassing Granville's 1936 record.

When Seabiscuit was moved to the Empire City track for the $20,000 Butler Handicap, it became evident that his own-folks were not the only horsemen who believed him to be the best stake racer on the American tracks. Owners and trainers of Thoroughbreds which are contending for championships are reluctant to start them in any race where they are almost certain to be beaten. Greater reluctance has seldom been shown than in the Butler Handicap of 1937. None of the big-name stake horses was started, and only five hopefuls went to the post with Seabiscuit. The handicapper believed their chances of winning so small that he slashed their loads sharply, trying to make a reasonably even race of it. Finance, the horse believed to have the best chance, was allowed to carry a load seven pounds lighter than Seabiscuit's. All the others were given an advantage of at least seventeen pounds. And Caught, the one considered to have almost no chance, was allowed twenty-four pounds — supposedly enough to give him an advantage of at least fifty lengths over Seabiscuit in the mile-and-a-sixteenth race.

Even with the tremendous weight handicaps against him, Seabiscuit went to the starting gate the odds-on favorite of the fans. And if ever a horse proved himself a champion in every fiber, the little outcast grandson of Man o' War proved it that day. He drew the number one post position, and shot straight forward at the bell, taking the lead close to the rail. But, from the outside starting position, Caught bolted like a streak of lightning, angled across the course, and shouldered him hard against the rail. As the crowd leaped to its feet, shouting, "Foul! Foul! Intentional foul!" Seabiscuit regained his stride and drove on, shoulder to shoulder with Caught. Within a dozen lengths, the frantic Caught bore in again, knocking him against the railing a second time. To escape further punishment, Red Pollard tried to pull back, but Seabiscuit set the crowd afire with a surge of power that left Caught a full length behind.

Electrifying as that burst of speed had been to the crowd, it was frightening to Red, for he could feel the unevenness of the rhythm. Baby was definitely favoring his left foreleg, but was in no mood to be held back. Driving with all his might, he pounded around the turn and up the backstretch, fighting off Caught's frantic effort to overtake him. Going into the far turn Caught fell back, but Thorson, with a nineteen-pound weight advantage, came rushing up to make his challenge. At the sound of the oncoming hoofbeats, Seabiscuit laid back his ears and called on the reserve of power that only a champion has. It was enough to take him into the head of the homestretch a length and a half in the lead, then he refused to give up an inch of it until he had flashed under the wire.

Seabiscuit's time for the Butler Handicap was two-fifths of a second slower than the track record, but is one of the most astonishing in race history, for every stride of the last mile and an eighth was taken under severe pain. When Caught forced him against the rail his left foreleg had been cut, and the suspensory tendon so badly sprained that it would have put any less courageous horse completely out of the race. Although

Seabiscuit didn't take a limping step as Red rode him back to the winner's circle, the fans, still furious at what they believed to be an intentional foul, sensed his injury and his courage. Standing and shouting themselves hoarse, they gave him the greatest ovation ever given a horse at Empire City.

By the next morning, sports writers throughout the entire country were acclaiming Seabiscuit as the handicap champion of the year, but among his own-folks there was only grief. The sprained suspensory tendon had become too painful to be touched, and it seemed impossible that even Tom Smith's amazing skill could heal the injury before the end of the racing season, if ever. Again Seabiscuit's gallant bid for greatness appeared to have been snatched away from him on the very brink of achievement. But this time the bid had been for far more than recognition as handicap champion of the year; it had been for recognition as one of the greatest race horses of all time.

In America, the greatest honor that any race horse can attain is the winning of the Triple Crown, and War Admiral, Man o' War's finest son, had just become the fourth horse in history ever to have won it. Seabiscuit's only chance of proving himself the greatest race horse of his time lay in defeating the Triple Crown winner, and until his injury that chance had seemed to be just around the corner, for War Admiral was expected to run in the Massachusetts Handicap.

No one can say how much of Seabiscuit's miraculous recovery was due to Tom Smith's skill and experience, to the devoted care given him by Ollie Olson and Red Pollard, or to his own marvelous recuperative power. Regardless of that, the tendon was sufficiently healed within two weeks that Tom believed it safe to enter him in the Yonkers Handicap. But it soon became evident that Seabiscuit's own-folks were the only ones who felt the least bit safe about the race. Only five horses were started against him, and the handicapper gave them from fifteen to twenty-two pounds advantage, saddling Seabiscuit with 129 pounds, the heaviest load ever carried in the twenty-eight runnings of the famous race. How he carried it on his injured leg is one of the marvels of American racing history. But the greatest marvel was that, with Red holding him in, he broke by two-fifths of a second a track record that had stood for twenty-three years. From that day on, there was only one horse in the world rated as worthy to race against him on even terms — War Admiral.

Following Seabiscuit's sensational winning of the Yonkers, all eyes in the racing world were turned toward the rich Massachusetts Handicap. There the winner's share of the purse would be more than $50,000, and it was expected that the two great champions would meet to contend for it. But to the disappointment of fans and horsemen alike, the showdown had to be postponed. When winning the Belmont Stake in June, War Admiral had overstepped and cut the heel of a forefoot. Although the injury had not been great, it had interfered with his training enough that he wasn't at his best, so Samuel Riddle, his owner, withdrew him from the Massachusetts classic.

The disappointment of the fans was small compared to that of Seabiscuit's own-folks. They had no doubts of his ability to beat his famous uncle, but they did have doubts as to how long his weakened forelegs could hold up under the strain of constant training and racing. In War Admiral's withdrawal from the classic it seemed more than probable that Seabiscuit's chances of proving himself among the all-time greats had again been snatched away.

As was expected, the handicapper required Seabiscuit to carry top weight of 130 pounds in the big race. Aneroid, his nearest rival for champion stakehorse honors, was given an advantage of two pounds, the other eleven starters from fourteen to thirty. Even though handicapped with twenty pounds more weight than average, Seabiscuit was made even-money favorite by the fans.

The day of the Massachusetts Handicap was hot, the track was dry and fast, and the grandstand was packed with a capacity crowd of 40,000 — most of the fans there for a first sight of Seabiscuit, the wonder horse. At the start he leaped into the lead, but Red slowed him on the first pass of the grandstand, letting Fair Knightess, an extremely fast mare, come up to set the pace. And how she set it! Flashing around the clubhouse turn and down the backstretch, she led Seabiscuit by two or three lengths, bringing the crowd to its feet with a thunderous roar.

Going into the far turn it appeared certain that Fair Knightess would steal the race, but Seabiscuit was simply being a gentleman; letting the lady enjoy some well-earned applause. In circling the end of the track, he moved up enough to lead her into the homestretch by a scant head. But there a complication arose. Caballero II, a highly regarded South American horse with a load of only 108 pounds, came rushing up to challenge for the lead.

Seabiscuit turned on just enough speed to romp under the wire, winner by a length, but Fair Knightess lacked the strength to withstand the South American's powerful charge. Even at that, she finished a close third and broke the previous track record.

As for Seabiscuit, breaking track records was an old story. With his $51,780 share of the purse, he was standing on the threshold of three world-wide racing records. His winnings for the year were already $142,030, more than four times Aneroid's, and only $2590 behind War Admiral's. From all parts of the country, track officials were offering purses ranging from $40,000 to $100,000, for a match race between the Triple Crown winner and the acknowledged king of the handicap division. Beyond that, Seabiscuit needed only one more victory to tie Discovery's record of winning eight important stake races in succession.

Although there were still several important stake

races to be run in the East, it was generally believed that Seabiscuit couldn't be heavily enough handicapped to be beaten by any horse except War Admiral. As a result, Top Row, Rosemont, and Time Supply were retired for the season, so they might be well rested and put into prime condition for the Santa Anita Handicap. Except for Seabiscuit's standing on the threshold of all-time greatness, he, too, would have been given a long rest in preparation for the Santa Anita classic — the prize most eagerly coveted for him by his own-folks. But in hope of a match race with War Admiral, it was decided to give him only a month's rest with light training, then enter him in one more stake race before returning him to California — either the $15,000-added Hawthorne Gold Cup to be run at Chicago on September 11, or the $25,000-added Narragansett Special, to be run at Pawtucket, Rhode Island, on the same date.

Soon after winning the Massachusetts Handicap, Seabiscuit was nominated for both the Special and the Gold Cup, for his own-folks were extremely anxious that he should meet War Admiral before returning to the West Coast. It was planned that, unless a match race were arranged in the meantime, Seabiscuit would be started in whichever of the races he could meet his famous rival for top honors of the year. If War Admiral were to be started in neither race, Seabiscuit would run in whichever offered him the lightest handicap weight.

When no match race had been arranged and it was announced that War Admiral would not run in the Hawthorne Gold Cup, Mr. Howard promised to start Seabiscuit in the Narragansett Special. He made the promise in hope of meeting with the Triple Crown winner, even though Seabiscuit would have to carry 132 pounds in the Special, and only 128 pounds in the Gold Cup. The choice was unfortunate.

On the night of September 10 a steady rain set in at Pawtucket, and on the day of the Narragansett Special the track was a sea of sloppy mud. War Admiral was not started, but because of Mr. Howard's promise he would not withdraw Seabiscuit, even though it meant risking severe injury and breaking his long string of successive triumphs, for with his heavy load he had little chance of winning in deep mud.

Only six horses went to the post for the Special: Aneroid, with a weight advantage of eleven pounds; Calumet Dick, one of the best mud runners in the country, with an advantage of seventeen; Snark, pasture mate of Seabiscuit's colthood days, with only 117 pounds aboard, and the two outsiders with lesser loads. Snark led most of the way, while Seabiscuit fought to stay close behind. Then in the homestretch, Calumet Dick splashed up to pass them both. With his double handicap of weight and mud, Seabiscuit was unable to meet the challenge, and had to take third place, three and a half lengths behind Calumet Dick. The defeat was doubly disappointing, since the Chicago track had been in excellent condition, and the time for the Hawthorne Gold Cup slow. No one doubted that Seabiscuit would have won it in a breeze if he had been there, making him the greatest successive winner of important stakes in racing history.

Still in hope of a match with War Admiral, Mr. Howard kept Seabiscuit in the East until the middle of November, when The Admiral was retired for the winter. But even though the match was not arranged, the time was not lost, for in those two months, Sunny. Jim Fitzsimmons' outcast entered the ranks of the all-time greats. He won three more big handicaps, and lost one by a scant nose, each time being handicapped to his rivals by fifteen pounds or more. When, at last, Seabiscuit boarded the train for California and his winter's rest, he took an impressive record with him: Champion money-winner of the year, with a total of $168,580 — well out in front of War Admiral, and breaking Man o' War's record by $2440. In addition, he had broken five track records and proved himself one of the greatest stake horses ever to have run on American tracks, for he had won eleven out of fifteen starts, all in topflight competition and under severe weight handicaps.

6

WHEN A Thoroughbred stallion has won an unquestionable championship, he is usually retired by the end of his fourth year. This is particularly true if his legs and joints are not entirely sound, for his value as a sire is considered to be much greater than the amount he could win thereafter. But when Seabiscuit was shipped back to California, Mr. Howard announced that he would be a "fighting champion" as long as he could be raced without serious injury to himself.

There were three reasons for the decision — three goals which his own-folks coveted for him. One of them was, of course, a match race with War Admiral. The second was the honor of winning the Santa Anita Handicap — an honor that had been snatched from him at the last moment, and which they were sure he could now win. The third was that he might prove himself the all-time stake-racing champion by topping Sun Beau's lifetime winnings of $376,744. This last seemed little more than an idle dream to other horse-men, for Seabiscuit's total winnings were only $210,000, he was known to have gimpy knees and tendons, and there was believed to be a jinx on break-ing Sun Beau's record. Phar Lap had died when within $40,000 of it, and the great Equipoise, the only horse ever to come closer, had broken down in the attempt. Besides, no race horse had ever won any-where near $165,000 after becoming five years old.

Seabiscuit's own-folks didn't argue the point, but laid their plans carefully. He was in excellent condi-tion and needed no complete rest, so he would be kept in light training, then sharpened up for the four big California handicaps. These four races would bring his total earnings well above Sun Beau's — if, as ex-pected, he won them all. If not, there would be plenty of lesser California races open to him, but he would be started only when track conditions and handicap weights were favorable. Shipping him to the East would not be risked again unless a definite meeting with War Admiral could be arranged.

All the Howard horses were raced in Mrs. Howard's name. For two years she had set her heart on winning the Santa Anita Handicap, and Mr. Howard was de-termined that she should not be disappointed a second

time. He had every confidence that Seabiscuit could win the classic if the track were dry and fast. But he couldn't be expected to win on a wet track while carrying top weight, and in early March rain might be expected in Southern California. To make doubly sure that Mrs. Howard should not be disappointed in her second try for the world's richest racing prize, Mr. Howard spent far more than the amount of that prize for horses to back up Seabiscuit. One of them was Fair Knightess, the powerful filly that had threatened to steal the Massachusetts Handicap, and that had proved herself capable of making fast time on a muddy track. Another was Chanceview, recognized as one of the best sloppy-track runners in the country. In addition, he imported six of the most promising Thoroughbreds available in Argentina.

With the San Francisco winter racing season just getting under way, Mr. Howard shipped his stable of twenty-two Thoroughbreds to Tanforan in mid-November. There Tom Smith, assisted by his son Jim, put them into training, and Red Pollard rode several of them during the early part of the meet. In the meantime, they were bringing Seabiscuit along carefully, getting him into perfect shape for the $10,000 Marchbank Handicap.

The big race was only a few days away when the Sun Beau jinx first made its appearance. Red Pollard, overanxious to win a race with Exhibit, was accused of rough riding, and the track stewards suspended him for the rest of the meet. Although loss of the prize would be a severe blow to Seabiscuit's chances of breaking Sun Beau's record, Mr. Howard withdrew him immediately from the Marchbank. It not only disappointed but angered the San Francisco fans and sports writers, who had been waiting a month to see their champion in action. They descended on Mr. Howard in droves, demanding that he let Seabiscuit run, and insisting that he could win with the poorest jockey at the track on him. "That I believe," Mr. Howard told them, "but if Red Pollard rides Seabiscuit I know he will bring him back without injury, and that is my chief concern. I will let him run when, and only when, conditions are favorable and Red can ride him."

The Santa Anita winter meet opened on Christmas, so the Howard stable was shipped there at once, with the intention that Red would ride Seabiscuit in the Christmas Stake. And again the jinx stepped in. The Tanforan stewards recommended to the California Race Board that Red's suspension be enforced throughout the state until the end of the year. Mr. Howard would not contest the recommendation, so again withdrew Seabiscuit, though it was conceded that he could have won in a breeze.

Light training will keep a race horse in good condition, and by increasing the length and speed of his workouts he can usually be brought into top racing form. But his competitive spirit can be honed to a slashing edge only through actual racing. Then too, some horses, particularly those with the keenest will to win, go stale unless they are raced at least once a month. Seabiscuit had been idle for more than a month and a half, and Tom Smith believed him to be badly in need of a race, so he was nominated for the New Year's Handicap, the first race in which Red could ride him. Then up popped the jinx: a dispute between Webb Everett, racing secretary at Santa Anita, and Mr. Howard.

Some owners in the East had been reluctant to

ship their horses to California, fearful that Seabiscuit would be given an advantage in his home state — that he would not be handicapped heavily enough to give their horses an equal chance of winning. Probably in an effort to reassure them, Everett required that the champion be weighted at 132 pounds for the New Year's Handicap — a load fourteen pounds greater than that of his nearest rival, and two more than he had been assigned for the Santa Anita classic. Since most of the horses nominated for the New Year's race were those that would run in the classic, Mr. Howard believed the two pounds — an additional handicap equal to four lengths — to be unfair, so took the only reasonable action open to him. He withdrew Seabiscuit from the race, announcing publicly that until after the Santa Anita Handicap the champion would be started in no race where he was weighted with more than 130 pounds.

Misunderstandings between two strong-willed men have caused great wars and changed the course of world history. The misunderstanding between Webb Everett and Charles Howard threatened to destroy Seabiscuit's bid for all-time greatness. Mr. Howard's first concern was for the welfare of his horse, but he was also determined that his wife should have the joy and honor on which she had set her heart: that of winning the Santa Anita Handicap. Only in the Narragansett Special had Seabiscuit been required to carry 132 pounds, and the strain of that race had nearly broken him down. Tom Smith was worried for fear he might go lame before the classic if weighted too heavily in the warm-up races, and Mr. Howard was simply refusing to run the risk.

It was well known that Seabiscuit would be the main attraction of the Santa Anita season, and that his popularity would bring huge crowds to see any race in which he ran. Webb Everett resented the public announcement that the champion would be started in no race where he was weighted with more than 130 pounds. He believed that Mr. Howard, through the popularity of his horse and public sentiment, was attempting to force his hand — and Webb Everett was no man to have his hand forced. In each of the warm-up races for the big classic he insisted on handicapping Seabiscuit with 132 pounds, and refused to schedule a suitable race without handicaps.

Never in the history of racing have owner, trainer, sportsmen, and fans been more anxious for a horse to race, but for nearly two months Webb Everett clung doggedly to his position, while Seabiscuit stood idle in his stall. And with every warm-up race he missed, his chances of winning the classic or topping Sun Beau's record became less and less. Then, on February 19th, the staggering blow was struck.

With Seabiscuit withdrawn, Mr. Howard and Tom Smith decided to start Fair Knightess in the $5000 San Carlos Handicap. And since it was the most important of the warm-up races, Red Pollard rode her.

Red held her behind He Did and Indian Broom until reaching the far turn, then brought her up quickly to slip through an opening between the two leaders. At the same moment Pompoon, the co-favorite with Seabiscuit for the $100,000 classic, was brought up fast on the outside. The four horses were flying shoulder to shoulder as they leaned into the curve at the end of the track.

Halfway around, Indian Broom bore out slightly from his position on the rail. It was just enough to put Fair Knightess into close quarters as she drove to pass He Did. Her forefoot touched his barely enough to make her stumble and fall. Before Red could jump clear, another horse piled into Fair Knightess from behind, rolling her completely over and crushing Red beneath her. By some miracle he wasn't killed, but suffered severe internal injuries, three broken ribs, and a broken collarbone. The doctors held out little hope that he would be able to ride again for a year.

With Red's accident, all hope for Seabiscuit's future seemed to be gone, for no other jockey had ever understood him and been able to bring out his best efforts. At first Mr. Howard and Tom Smith considered withdrawing Seabiscuit from the classic, but it didn't seem fair that he should be denied his chance, so they set about to find the best possible jockey for him. In making their decision, Tom and his boss had their only known disagreement. Tom favored Georgie Woolf, but

Mr. Howard favored Sonny Workman — and final choice rests with the owner.

As soon as Sonny had been chosen, Tom Smith put him and Seabiscuit into intense training, for success in the big race could be expected only if horse and rider learned to understand and have complete confidence in each other. And, as always, Tom scheduled two sessions on the training track each day; an unimpressive get-acquainted one at dawn, and a sharpening-up one for both Seabiscuit and Sonny after the stopwatch birds had gone home. When Tom didn't have Workman in training on the track, Red Pollard had him in training at his bedside in the hospital, telling him every secret but one that he had learned about Baby, and how to call on him for his best effort. The secret he held back was one that he didn't dare let any other jockey know, for it would ruin Seabiscuit as a race horse. Even in the hardest drive, he would stop whenever he heard the command, "Whoa!"

For the $7500 San Antonio Handicap, to be run on the Saturday before the classic, Webb Everett relented and assigned Seabiscuit a handicap weight of 130 pounds. With this being the last tune-up for the Santa Anita Handicap, thirteen horses were started, all of them candidates for the big race. Seabiscuit drew the number five position in the starting gate, and Sonny Workman got him away to a poor start. At the first turn he was in fifth place, blocked behind the leaders. Workman was unable to get him free through the backstretch, and he trailed into the homestretch by three and a half lengths. Then Seabiscuit took over without help from his jockey. In a driving finish he overtook Indian Broom and Time Supply but Aneroid's handicap advantage of twelve pounds was a bare shade too much for him. His closest stake rival of the past summer beat him to the wire by a scant nose.

Tom Smith was furious at the ride Workman had given Seabiscuit, and convinced Mr. Howard to let Georgie Woolf ride him in the big race. The choice was a happy one, for Woolf, Red Pollard, and Tom were three of a kind. They all had started out as cowboys, gained their first experience with Thoroughbreds on the bush-league circuit, and been friends for years. From the first time the famous jockey mounted The Biscuit, as he called him, he believed the little bay stallion to be the finest race horse in the world, and Seabiscuit understood and gave him his best. During the week before the Santa Anita Handicap, Georgie spent hours at Red's bedside, and when the horses went to the post he knew all he needed to know.

Eighteen horses went to the post for the classic, Seabiscuit carrying ten pounds more than the other favorites (Aneroid and Pompoon) and thirty pounds — equal to a handicap of sixty lengths — more than Stagehand, the horse considered to have the least chance in the race. Even with his tremendous weight handicap and Aneroid's having beaten him in the San

Antonio, the fans made Seabiscuit their favorite, at nine-to-five. At the gate he stood quietly in stall twelve, poised and waiting for the bell. On his left, Pompoon danced nervously, while on his right Count Atlas, a sixty-to-one shot with no business in such a race, reared excitedly.

At the bell Seabiscuit sprang straight and fast from his stall, but had barely cleared it before Count Atlas lunged into him, knocking him nearly to his knees. Before he could recover, the pace setters were ten lengths down the track, and Count Atlas was squarely in front of him, pulled nearly to a stop by his equally excited jockey, Johnny Adams. Furious at the interference, Georgie Woolf swung his whip high, and slashed it down across the confused Adams' back, driving him and his half-crazed mount out of the way.

As they swept past the frenzied crowd in the grandstand Seabiscuit was a dozen lengths behind the pace setters, driving with all his might to make up for lost ground. Woolf held him tight to the rail, saving every possible inch as they rounded the clubhouse turn. Once in the backstretch, they began cutting down on the tiring laggards, Georgie threading the needle through the pack with uncanny skill. By the time they had reached the far turn, Woolf had piloted Seabiscuit into sixth place, had him in the clear, and called on him for his best.

In the grandstand the crowd was on its feet and in a tumult of excitement. Above the deafening roar Clem

McCarthy's voice crackled over the radio like machine-gun fire: "Seabiscuit! He's coming through! He's cutting the others down like a whirlwind! He's got Aneroid now! They're going into the far turn! He's taking the lead! It's Seabiscuit and Aneroid again! They're head and head around the turn! Pompoon is moving but is not getting up! I don't think he will get up! But look! Stagehand is moving! He's coming like a wild horse! He's catching the leader! *Look out for him!*

"They're turning into the stretch! Seabiscuit has taken the lead! Aneroid is second! Now he's beginning to falter! Aneroid is done! It's Seabiscuit and Stagehand! They're coming away! It's all between them! Seabiscuit still leads by a head! They're almost here! Stagehand is running stronger. He's headed Seabiscuit. But Seabiscuit won't yield. How he tries! But it's Stagehand! Stagehand by inches! Not more than four of them!"

In his column the next morning Clem wrote: "Seabiscuit, how great a horse — and how unfortunate! What kind of a race is it that makes such things possible? The pitting of a horse burdened with 130 pounds against one carrying an even hundred! Where are the reason, equity, the sportsmanship, involved? The money went to a three-year-old with a feather on his back. But nothing can ever give him the glory or take it away from the little horse with 130 pounds. A brilliant race, a wonderful race, a magnificent, a thrilling, a record-breaking race. Pile up the adjectives as you will. But one in which the best horse was unjustly beaten."

Clem McCarthy, with consummate skill, had put into words what every horseman, sports writer, and racing fan in the country knew. The only thing he had missed was that Seabiscuit was hoodooed by the Sun Beau jinx. Twice, through no fault of his own, the richest racing prize in the world had been snatched from him by inches. And that difference — barely a foot in both races combined — had cost him $160,000 in winnings, enough to top Sun Beau's record. But the jinx had only begun to play its pranks.

7

On the day that Seabiscuit lost the Santa Anita Handicap, War Admiral won the $50,000 Widener Challenge Cup at Hialeah Park in Florida. The two races splashed the names of Man o' War's superb son and grandson in headlines on every sports page in the United States, fanning the clamor for a match race between the two great champions to white heat. From Florida, Sunny Jim Fitzsimmons added fuel to the flames by making the statement that he was inclined to believe Seabiscuit would win if a match race between the two were ever run. Arlington Park at Chicago and Belmont Park at New York immediately offered a $100,000 winner-take-all purse for "the match race of the century."

Excitement among horsemen, fans, and sports writers reached fever pitch. Charles Howard and Samuel Riddle were besieged with wires and telephone calls. Both owners agreed to the match, but each made his agreement provisional. Mr. Riddle demanded that War Admiral be required to carry no more than 126 pounds, and that the race be at a mile and a quarter, on a fast, dry track. Anxious as Mr. Howard was for the match, he demanded that it should not be run until Red Pollard was again able to ride Seabiscuit, and that the weight carried by both horses must be equal.

At Mr. Howard's announcement gloom settled over the racing world, for it was well known that the doctors had said Red would be unable to ride before the end of the year. And there was little doubt that War Admiral would be retired from racing before that time. But Red Pollard was made of as tough stuff as Seabiscuit himself, and proved the doctors to be wrong by at least eight months. As March came to a close he was able to go to Mexico to watch Baby win the Agua Caliente Handicap, and was positive that he could ride within a month. The wires began humming again, and the match race was finally agreed upon. It was to be run at Belmont Park on Memorial Day for a purse of $100,000, and both horses were to carry 126 pounds.

In mid-April Seabiscuit was shipped to San Francisco, where Georgie Woolf rode him, carrying 130 pounds, to another track record in winning the $15,000

116

Bay Meadows Handicap. A week later The Biscuit's private car rolled away for the three-thousand-mile trip to Belmont Park. Riding with him were Pumpkin and Ollie Olson, and the back half of the car was piled high with California oats, hay, and rice straw. In the next Pullman car, where they could keep a constant eye on the champion, were Tom Smith and Red Pollard — his chest and shoulders still bound in adhesive tape.

Never had Seabiscuit been in as fine condition as when he was unloaded at Belmont Park. For the first time in his life his bay coat was dappled — the sure sign of perfect condition in a horse. The muscles of his hindquarters bulged with power, and the tendons of his knobby-kneed forelegs were as taut as fiddle strings. His only possible fault was the few extra pounds he had gained during the trip, but those would quickly disappear with training.

Less than two years before, Seabiscuit had left New York as a friendless outcast. When he returned for the match race an admiring throng waited for him to be led from his private car, cameras clicked, flash bulbs sparkled like fireflies, and sports writers filled their columns with his praises:

On April 25, Seabiscuit arrived in New York from San Francisco. Almost all of Man o' War's descendants are big horses, but both Seabiscuit and War Admiral are rather small. Otherwise they are not at all

alike. War Admiral is fiery, untractable, tempera-
mental. Seabiscuit is amiable, well-poised, and very
intelligent.

He knows he's good, too, but he hasn't forgotten
the days when he was next to nobody. Step up to his
stall to look him over and he comes forward to *look
you over*. Whisper sweet nothings to him and he
perks up his ears like a co-ed on a summer night.
And he's a cameraman's sweetheart. Flash bulbs
exploding all over the place arouse his curiosity instead of his heels.

The Admiral, pride of the East, buck-jumped,
reared, and tossed his saddle off twice before they
finally got him settled down. The Biscuit came
sauntering up like he owned the place, and after
jockey Red Pollard had climbed on his back he
struck a pose and held it for close to five minutes. He
didn't ripple a muscle when the movie machines
began whirring in his face. Seems to know that
facing the lens is part of the job of being a champion.

After talking with and about Seabiscuit, you go
away agreeing with trainer Tom Smith. If you
didn't like a horse like that you wouldn't be much
of a horse lover. You wouldn't like much of anything else, for that matter.

For three weeks, while the rival camps trained their
champions for the duel, sports writers all over the country beat the drums for "the greatest sports event of the

century." Plans were made to bring Man o' War from Kentucky to see his son and grandson match strides for the race-horse supremacy of the world. Box seats were selling for fabulous prices, thousands of orders had been turned down, and a crowd of 75,000, the largest ever to see a racing event in America, was expected to overflow the grounds. Hundreds of thousands of dollars had already been wagered on the outcome.

Tom Smith and Red Pollard went at Seabiscuit's training in their usual careful manner, and for the match he needed a lot of special schooling. War Admiral hadn't lost a race since becoming a three-year-old, and the pattern of every one had been the same. He was always first away, then quickly opened so great a lead that he could never be caught. Evening after evening Tom and Red put Seabiscuit through his schooling over and over again, teaching him to break from the starting gate with every atom of speed he could muster.

By the Monday before Memorial Day both Tom and Red were convinced that Seabiscuit could break from the gate with greater speed than War Admiral had ever shown. Then the Sun Beau jinx and the abuse of his colthood days caught up with him. His knee joints became inflamed and swollen. To continue his training before the inflammation was cured might cripple him permanently. To race him without that final week's sharpening would be unfair to the thousands of fans who had bet on him. After a meeting between owners and track officials, it was decided that the match must be called off, and no postponement date could be agreed upon.

The only possibility of the two great champions meeting appeared to be in the Massachusetts Handicap, to be run on June 29. War Admiral was already nominated for the $50,000 classic, and Mr. Howard nominated Seabiscuit immediately, confident that Tom Smith could get him back into racing form within a month.

As always in the past, Seabiscuit's injury responded rapidly to Tom's treatment. By early June the inflammation in his knees was completely cured, so he was shipped to Boston for the big Suffolk Downs race — and his jinx followed close on his heels. Again Tom and Red put him back into training, worked off the fat he had put on during two weeks of idleness, and brought him carefully back into top-notch racing condition. One morning when Red came back to the barn from a workout, a friend asked him to ride a colt with which he was having trouble. As a favor, Red agreed, although he hadn't regained his full strength. The colt, completely spoiled and unmanageable, bolted into the rail, shattering Red's leg above and below the knee and tearing the flesh away from the bone. This time the doctor told him he would never ride again, that he would be fortunate if he ever walked.

For nearly two years Red Pollard's one ambition in life had been to ride Baby to all-time greatness; to prove to the world that he was a greater race horse than even his famous grandsire. And now there could be no doubt that his ambition was as hopelessly shattered as his leg. Red wasted no time in grieving for himself; only for the horse that he loved above all else. He had no fear that Seabiscuit wouldn't give Georgie Woolf his very best — he had proved that he would do that in the Santa Anita Handicap. Red's fear was of training injuries.

Steel itself can stand only so much stress, and Baby's bone and sinew were coming nearer to the limit of their endurance with every hard training workout. If he were pushed a hair's breadth beyond that limit he might easily be crippled for life. But if, as in his training for the match race, the injury could be detected in time, it could be cured before any lasting damage was done. And Red knew that he alone could detect the symptoms of overstress in time. The empathy between himself and Seabiscuit had become so strong that, through rhythm of motion alone, he could sense the slightest twinge of pain, the faintest sign of fatigue or soreness. Wizard that Tom Smith was, he couldn't possibly detect those earliest symptoms from the ground. And skillful jockey that Georgie Woolf was, he couldn't detect them from the saddle. Worse still, Seabiscuit was so overflowing with courage that he would hide his injuries, and, if allowed, would drive himself beyond the limits of reasonable fatigue.

With the match race called off and Red Pollard hopelessly crippled, Mr. Howard's first impulse was to retire Seabiscuit from racing immediately, but the pressures against it were tremendous. In the first place, the soreness was entirely gone from Seabiscuit's knees, he was rounding into the best racing condition of his life, and Tom Smith was positive he could win the Massachusetts Handicap from War Admiral if Georgie Woolf could be secured as his jockey.

Next to winning the Santa Anita Handicap, Mr. Howard's fondest ambition for his great champion was that he have his chance to prove himself the master of War Admiral, and the Suffolk Downs classic appeared to be his only possible chance of proving it. Then too, the attention of the entire racing world was now centered in the Massachusetts classic, for it was considered to be strictly a contest between the two champions. Boston was already thronged with horsemen and racing enthusiasts from all over the country, hundreds of thousands had been wagered, and excitement had reached the boiling point. If Seabiscuit were again withdrawn from a meeting with his famous rival, his backers would be chagrined and furious, for they would have no choice but to believe it an acknowledgment of War Admiral's superiority.

In spite of the pressure, Mr. Howard would have withdrawn Seabiscuit if he had been unable to secure

Georgie Woolf as his rider. Even then, when the weather became threatening on the day before the classic, he made a public statement to the sports writers: "If the track is fast tomorrow, he'll go. If the track is soupy, even with rain falling, he'll go. But if the track is what they call heavy, with the footing made up of sticky mud which pulls at his legs and bad knees, he won't start. That would be unfair to him and he's earned his right to a fair break."

Threatening as the weather had been, the rain clouds blew over. The day of the Massachusetts Handicap dawned bright and clear, and the track was in excellent condition. So was Seabiscuit. By sunrise Tom Smith and Georgie Woolf had him out for his final tune-up, and he knew as well as they that it was the day of the big race. From the moment they reached the track he was so eager to run at top speed that Woolf had to keep him under constant restraint. After he was thoroughly warmed up, Tom let Georgie open him up for a burst of all-out speed, then they put him through his final schooling at the starting gate. In this race the getaway would be of the utmost importance, for Seabiscuit would be starting from the gate, while War Admiral, because of his unruliness, would start from outside.

Tom's plan was to put Seabiscuit through a few lightning-fast starts, letting him run no more than a half-furlong at top speed before being brought back.

If Red Pollard had been in the saddle, the training would have gone exactly as planned, for he had taught Baby to stop at the command, "Whoa." But that was the one secret Red never dared tell another jockey. That morning Seabiscuit broke from the gate faster than ever before, and his will to run was so overpowering that Georgie Woolf, skillful though he was, could barely pull him in at the end of a full furlong. As a result, Tom cut down on the number of starts he had planned, for he could see they were unnecessary, and he didn't want to risk the possibility of strain. Seabiscuit had undoubtedly reached the sharpest racing form of his career, and all he needed in order to beat War Admiral was a chance to run against him.

Now that the long-awaited showdown with War Admiral was only hours away, Tom Smith would take no chance of an oversight, slip-up, or the possibility of tampering. Following the workout, he himself walked Seabiscuit until he was thoroughly cooled out, made sure there was no tender spot or swelling in any joint or tendon, then put on the knee braces and bandaged each leg with liniment and cotton padding. With the bandages bound just snugly enough to keep the liniment warm, but to allow for free circulation of blood, Tom seated himself at the stall doorway. There he would sit, guarding Son and watching his every movement until time to take the bandages off, a few minutes before saddling time. As the forenoon wore on, Tom noticed that Seabiscuit was restless, but that was not unusual on the day of a race, so he paid little attention to it.

Long before noon the early birds began pouring into the Suffolk Downs grandstand, even though the classic would not be run before five o'clock. By 4:30 nearly 70,000 fans and horsemen thronged the stands, clubhouse, and infield. Special wires had been installed in the press box, and sportscasters from every part of the country were already broadcasting preliminary news of the "race of the century." In front of the betting windows a milling mob of bettors jostled and pushed, most of them anxious to lay a two-, five-, or ten-dollar wager on the nose of one or the other of the two famous champions. Then pandemonium broke out in the steward's office. Mr. Howard and Tom Smith had just come in to scratch Seabiscuit from the race, saying that when his bandages were taken off Tom had found a foreleg hot with fever, and that he was certain the tendon would bow if the horse were allowed to run.

Steward Tom Thorpe had every reason to be angry. Only the day before, Mr. Howard had announced publicly that Seabiscuit would run if the track were in good shape. It was because of that announcement and the good weather that the tremendous crowd had paid its money to get into Suffolk Downs, positive of seeing the greatest race between two champions that had been run since Man o' War met Sir Barton. If Seabiscuit were withdrawn now, the fans would be justifiably furious, convinced that they had been intentionally bilked out of their money. Furthermore, the deadline for scratching from the classic was already past by several minutes. Tom Thorpe insisted that Seabiscuit be started, regardless of his condition. Tom Smith insisted just as vehemently that he wouldn't let his horse go to the post; that if he were raced in his present condition he would be completely ruined for life.

Mr. Howard at last brought reason to the argument by pointing out that it would be more unfair to the fans to let Seabiscuit run than to withdraw him. If his tendon were to bow during the race he couldn't possibly win, and his backers would have been cheated. After half an hour's discussion, it was agreed to leave the matter up to Dr. Eugene Bradley and Dr. C. A. Boutelle, the state and track veterinarians. If, after examination, they believed that Seabiscuit's condition would not seriously handicap him in the race he would have to be started, regardless of Tom Smith's opinion.

The examination required no more than a glance, then both veterinarians reported that Seabiscuit would never race again, that the injury to his tendon was beyond any possibility of curing. As was expected, the crowd became furious with disappointment and anger

when the announcement was made on the public ad-
dress system. The track announcer had to shout
louder and louder as the boos increased. At the end
of his broadcast he literally screamed, *"and this is
positively the truth!"*

Fighting and knocking each other down, the fans
that had wagered on Seabiscuit rushed for the betting
windows, determined to switch their bets to War Admiral before it was too late. So great was the rush
that the odds were driven down to forty cents on the
dollar by the time the horses reached the post, but the
lucky fans were those who didn't reach the windows.
The time of the Massachusetts Handicap was three
and a half seconds slower than Seabiscuit's time the
previous year — and War Admiral finished a poor
fourth, tiring badly in the homestretch under his 126-
pound load.

The bowing of a tendon is due to fatigue, and Red
Pollard's fear had proved justified. There could be no
doubt that in his morning workout, Seabiscuit had
been allowed to overdo, bringing on the injury.
Neither was there any doubt that he would have been
permanently disabled if allowed to run in the classic.
But though Tom Smith had given the learned veterinarians no argument, he was far from being in agreement with them. Time and again he had been obliged
to halt Son's training because a tendon had become
inflamed and threatened to bow, and this injury was

no worse than some of the others had been. With it caught in time, Tom knew he could put Seabiscuit into racing condition again. Of course, the weakened tendon could never be entirely cured, the original damage had been done too long ago, but it could be strengthened and the swelling reduced before it became crippling.

Most men having as valuable a stallion as Seabiscuit had become would have retired him from racing immediately. But Mr. Howard had implicit faith in Tom Smith's judgment and magical healing skill. When Tom told him that he would again have Seabiscuit ready to start in the next year's Santa Anita Handicap, and believed he could get him ready for the Hollywood Gold Cup, Mr. Howard wired at once to request information on handicap weights. The reply was as discouraging as the other ill-fortune that had befallen the champion. The Hollywood racing secretary went Webb Everett one better, insisting that Seabiscuit must carry 133 pounds if he were to start in the $50,000 handicap. Even though the race was barely two weeks — though more than three thousand miles — away, Tom told Mr. Howard to make the entry, that he would have Seabiscuit ready to run and carry the excessive weight.

Tom Smith was as good as his word. He not only had the champion ready but in tiptop shape, in spite of the train ride across the entire country. While Seabiscuit's California fans — who, a couple of weeks before, had grieved at the news that his racing days were ended — went berserk in their excitement, he flashed under the wire to win the Hollywood Gold Cup by a length and a half. To prove that his racing days were far from ended, he not only broke the track record but added $37,150 to his winnings. Less than a month later he broke the track record at Del Mar, winning another $25,000 in a match race with Bing Crosby's great South American import, Ligaroti.

8

Any possibility of a match between Seabiscuit and War Admiral had been given up when the veterinarians made their report at Suffolk Downs. But with his victories in the Gold Cup and against Ligaroti, horsemen and fans alike hailed him as The Iron Horse, and again the telegraph wires began to click. It was proposed that the $100,000 "race of the century" be run as a special feature of the fall meeting at Belmont Park. With War Admiral already nominated to run there in the October 1 Jockey Gold Cup race, Mr. Riddle agreed to the match, but insisted that it be run on a day when the track was fast, that War Admiral carry no more than 126 pounds, and that either owner withdrawing his horse pay the other a forfeit of $25,000.

All hope of topping Sun Beau's record had appeared to be gone when it became necessary to withdraw Seabiscuit from both the Memorial Day match race and the Massachusetts Handicap, but it was quickly revived by Mr. Riddle's agreement. If the weakened knees and tendons would hold up through another long trip East and a sharp training program, Seabiscuit's own-folks were positive he could beat War Admiral. And $100,000, added to his California winnings for the year, would take him well beyond Sun Beau's record, making him the champion money-winning race horse of all time. Mr. Howard was anxious enough for the contest that he agreed to all of Mr. Riddle's demands, requiring only that both horses carry the same weight. So, in early September, Seabiscuit was again shipped to New York — and the Sun Beau jinx rode in the car with him.

September was a rainy month in New York, the Belmont track was slow, and to meet Mr. Riddle's requirements the match had to be repeatedly postponed. While waiting for the track to dry, Seabiscuit was entered in the Manhattan Handicap, the only September race at Belmont for which he was eligible. He was assigned, as he should have been, a twenty-pound handicap above his rivals. Even so, he could have won easily on a reasonably dry track, but on the day of the race it rained all forenoon, the track was ankle-deep in mud, and the best he could do was to take third place, three lengths behind the winner. Although, under the conditions, he ran an excellent race, his loss was enough to cool the New York fans' enthusiasm for a match race with War Admiral, and the bookmakers began offering even money that it would never be run.

Except for two circumstances, the bookmakers might have been right in their guess, and Mr. Riddle might have retired War Admiral as the unquestionable champion. The first of these was that Mrs. Howard's niece had recently married Alfred Gwynne Vanderbilt, an owner of the Pimlico track at Baltimore. The second was that, a week after losing at Belmont, Seabiscuit won the Havre de Grace Handicap. In doing so, he beat Menow by three and a half lengths — and Menow was the horse that had defeated War Admiral by four lengths in the Massachusetts Handicap. Mr. Vanderbilt was a close friend of both Samuel Riddle and Charles Howard, and knew that each man honestly believed his horse to be far the superior. Although any possibility of a $100,000 purse was gone, he brought the two owners together and suggested that the match be run at Pimlico for a much smaller purse.

Unless Seabiscuit had beaten Menow, and unless Samuel Riddle had been one of the finest sportsmen in America, the meeting would never have taken place, for he had everything to lose and very little to gain by a matching of the two champions. A Thoroughbred stallion that is the unquestionable champion when retired is worth infinitely more as a sire than an ex-champion. And War Admiral was generally considered to be the unquestionable champion. Many horsemen believed that Seabiscuit had been withdrawn from the Memorial Day match because his trainer feared defeat, rather than because of injury. They believed the same of his withdrawal from the Massachusetts Handicap, since the tendon had given no trouble afterwards. Beyond that, Samuel Riddle had agreed to a meeting at Belmont, and it was no fault of his that the track had been too muddy to fulfill the requirements.

Other horsemen would have overlooked the fact that Menow had defeated War Admiral and then been soundly beaten by Seabiscuit, but Samuel Riddle wouldn't. That was the only black mark against War Admiral's record, and Mr. Riddle was determined to erase it. For twenty years Man o' War had been the pride of the old sportsman's life, but he, too, was growing old, and when his finest son replaced him as the monarch of Glen Riddle Farm he must do so with as clean a record.

Even though Samuel Riddle was anxious that the black mark be erased, he was fully aware of the tremendous risk he would be taking, and in exchange demanded that War Admiral have what he believed to be a considerable advantage. He insisted that the distance of the race be one and three-sixteenths miles, that the track be fast, that War Admiral carry no more than 120 pounds, and that the start be made from a walk-up to a line.

Since Mr. Riddle readily agreed that Seabiscuit should also carry 120 pounds, the only real advantage he demanded was the walk-up start, but that alone might be enough to win the race before it was more than begun. Seabiscuit had never been started except from a gate, and War Admiral had seldom started from within one. He was frightfully nervous at the post, and became unmanageable if confined to a gate stall. As a result, he was always put outside, and the rules of racing required that he be given a one-length handicap to offset the advantage. Even so, he had the ability to get away from a standing start so fast that he always made up the handicap with his first three or four strides. His trainer knew that if he were already in motion he could get away even faster, so the walk-up start was demanded both to save the length and give him a flying getaway.

Mr. Howard realized how great an advantage was being demanded, but he also realized how great a risk Mr. Riddle was running in agreeing to the match at all. Then too, he must accept any terms he could get if Seabiscuit were to have his chance, for War Admiral definitely would be retired at the end of the year. It was finally agreed that the contest would be held on the first November day when the track was dry enough to be considered fast, and the purse would be $15,000, winner-take-all. If either horse were withdrawn, its owner would forfeit $5000.

With the long anticipated meeting between the two champions definitely set, Tom Smith and Georgie Woolf put Seabiscuit into the most careful training of his career. Whenever the track was reasonably dry they had him out morning and afternoon, but never allowed him to approach the point of fatigue. After a warm-up canter and a short breeze of speed, he was schooled over and over at the walk-up start, for that was where War Admiral was expected to have his greatest advantage.

So that the practice starts might be as much as possible like that in the race, Tom made himself a gong. Then, for their first lessons, he had Georgie Woolf wear spurs. With Tom's hand poised over the gong, and with Georgie's heels pointed at Seabiscuit's sides, he was walked up to the starting line. The moment he reached it, Tom hit the gong, Georgie pricked with the spurs, and at the unexpected sting Seabiscuit nearly leaped out from under his saddle. Although horses have little or no reasoning power, they have an extremely keen sense of association. After three or four of these starts, the spurs were no longer necessary, for Seabiscuit had come to associate the sound of the gong with the sting of the spurs. He would walk up to the line quietly, but the instant Tom struck the gong he was away like an arrow from a sprung bow.

During the last week of his training, Tom played another trick on Son. He was never allowed to start without an extremely fast sprinter beside him, and he was never allowed to run out the first furlong. This would have discouraged almost any other Thoroughbred, but not Seabiscuit. His determination to win was so keen that it angered him to be pulled back when he was in a fight for the lead, and the oftener Georgie pulled him back the angrier he became. By the end of the week he was leaving the walk-up line like a flash of lightning, and it took every ounce of Georgie's strength to slow him down before the furlong post was reached.

Tom Smith was at last convinced that he had Son as ready as he could ever be for the greatest race of his career, but there was still one thing to be done. And in that one thing Tom bowed to the only man on earth who understood Seabiscuit better than he did. Red Pollard was in the hospital at Winthrop, Massachusetts, where, after four and a half months, the surgeons were still trying to rebuild his shattered leg. Tom had Georgie Woolf call Red on the phone and get his advice on riding the race.

Even with the excellent training starts Seabiscuit had made, Woolf expected War Admiral to set the early pace as he had done in every race he had run, but Red told him, "Don't let him do it! You set the pace and let the Admiral come up to you when he makes his bid, then pull away. Baby might loaf sometimes when he's in front and thinks he's got a race in the bag, but once a horse gives him the old look in the eye he begins to run to parts unknown, and he gets gamer and gamer the tougher it gets. Give him a chance to snort that challenge of his and he'll make a rear admiral out of War Admiral, I know that."

The next thing heard from Red was in a wire, addressed to Mr. Howard at the Pimlico track on the day of the race. "Please bet two hundred for me. Our horse will win by five. Pollard."

Red Pollard's confidence wasn't shared by the railbirds, or by the heavy-betting horsemen of the East. By post time they had driven the odds against Seabiscuit to four-to-one. Part of the reason can be seen in Grantland Rice's eyewitness report in his "High Spots of 1938."

As the two great horses of the American turf came out before the packed-in crowd, War Admiral looked like the Champion. His head was up, his feet were twinkling. He was ready to run. He was far and away the most impressive looking Thoroughbred.

Seabiscuit looked to be just a little sleepy. His head was down and he was merely drifting along, but he looked up once as if to count the crowds and see whether or not he had his full quota . . . On the way to the post War Admiral looked to be more and more the champion. Every move he made carried class. I began to wonder whether they could wake up Seabiscuit before the race started . . . He didn't look

like any winner as he passed the stands . . . Seabiscuit
had been over the hard way too many times before
. . . the crowd suddenly seemed to feel a deep pity
for this old campaigner.

Grantland Rice, as few other sports writers could do, had captured and put on paper the exact mood of the huge crowd that sat in awed silence, as if watching the funeral procession of a beloved old friend. Mrs.

Howard couldn't force herself to look, but sat with her program covering her tear-filled eyes. She had pinned her St. Christopher medal to Seabiscuit's saddle pad, and could only wait for the result with faith and anguish. As well as she knew Tom Smith, she couldn't realize that this was no more than a demonstration of his wizardry; that he had Seabiscuit completely relaxed, supremely confident of his ability to win, and conserving every ounce of his energy. And more of Silent Tom's wizardry was soon to be revealed.

George Cassidy, recognized as the best walk-up starter in the country, had been brought to Pimlico from New York, to make sure that both horses should have an equal break at the getaway. But as Tom Smith expected, Cassidy had brought no starting gong with him, and there was only one at the track that was not attached to a starting gate. When, before going to the starting line, Cassidy asked for a portable gong, Tom brought out the one he had made — the tone of which Seabiscuit had learned to associate with the sting of spurs.

With a judge and timers standing by, and with Tom Smith's gong attached to the rail, George Cassidy stood waiting at the starting line as the horses came toward the post. Out in front, War Admiral bobbed his head and pranced proudly, his nerves vibrating like a hummingbird's wings in his eagerness for the battle. Far behind, Seabiscuit poked along like a little boy on his way to school when he didn't want to go. While Charley Kurtsinger, War Admiral's jockey, held him, rearing and dancing at the starting line, George Cassidy called irritably to Georgie Woolf, "Bring him up! Bring him up!"

"Got to warm him up first," Georgie called back, putting Seabiscuit into a lazy canter.

"Bring him up; it's post time!" Cassidy ordered.

"Sorry, Mr. Cassidy, I've got orders from the trainer, and I'll have to do what he told me," Georgie sang out, then rode Seabiscuit right on past the line.

There was nothing Cassidy could do but let him go, for a trainer is entitled to demand that his horse be warmed up just before the start of a race. Tom Smith had no interest in warming up Seabiscuit; he'd been ready to run his race from the moment he stepped onto the track. Tom's interest was in the unruly War Admiral, his nerves trained to a feather edge for a lightning-fast getaway. The longer he could be held poised on the brink of battle, the more that feather edge would flutter — and fluttering nerves are exhausting.

While War Admiral fidgeted, danced, and reared, Georgie Woolf loped Seabiscuit far around the end of the track, turned him, and loped him back at the same lazy gait. After waiting for Georgie to come back, Charley Kurtsinger swung in beside him, and the two champions walked toward the starting line — Seabiscuit sauntering along on the outside, and War Admiral forging ahead along the rail. Nearing the line, War Admiral swung out nervously, and George Cassidy sent them back to try the walk-up a second time. It was no better than the first, so he sent them back again. This was the start Georgie Woolf had been waiting for. He crouched a bit lower over Biscuit's neck, and brought him up in perfect stride with War Admiral. That slight extra crouch had telegraphed to Seabiscuit all he needed to know. This was it! At the familiar sound of Tom's gong, he shot from the line like a frightened gazelle. And, as he went, Georgie's whip slashed down — just once — across his rump.

In a mile-and-three-sixteenths race at Pimlico, the first quarter post stands between the bleachers and the grandstand, with the finish line (after one circling of the track) between the grandstand and the clubhouse. In this way, the horses passed bleachers and grandstand twice, but only the fans in the bleachers — always the most rabid — could get a good view of the start. All through the preliminaries the two-dollar boys with a ticket on poor old Seabiscuit sat glumly. Those with a mutuel ticket on War Admiral chewed their gum listlessly, waiting for the race to be over, so they could go back to the windows and collect their fifty-cent winnings. For an instant after the gong sounded there was an awed silence. Then the bleacher fans leaped to their feet, screeching like Indians on the warpath. At the head of the homestretch they had glimpsed the bright red Howard colors — the wrong ones — bobbing out in front.

In that one crack of the whip, Georgie Woolf had told Biscuit this was for keeps — that there would be no pulling in at the furlong pole. And Seabiscuit, frustrated to fury for the past few days, poured every atom of that fury into his drive away from the line. As startled as the fans in the bleachers, Charley Kurtsinger flailed his whip as though he were beating a carpet, but War Admiral couldn't match the whirlwind getaway. By the time the end of the bleachers was reached, Biscuit was a full length in the lead, and winging. Behind, Charley Kurtsinger slashed mercilessly, still losing ground but trying to bring War Admiral up to the killing pace.

On past the screaming fans in the bleachers they flew, Georgie Woolf peeking back to see if he'd gained enough room to cross over and take the rail. A length and a half in front, he made his cross-over as they swept past the wildly cheering crowd in the grandstand. Close against the rail, and with Seabiscuit in full flight to hold his lead, they passed the tense, applauding celebrities in the clubhouse. There Mrs. Howard buried her face against the railing of her box, not daring to look up. Samuel Riddle, well past his eightieth birthday, stood like a chunky stone image, his field glasses fixed on his beloved son of Man o' War; on his horse that never since he was a two-year-

143

old had breathed dust in the early stages of a race.

On around the clubhouse turn and into the backstretch, the nephew and his year-younger uncle held their positions like spokes in a whirling wheel, both riders crouched low but neither using the whip. With the first excitement of Seabiscuit's unexpected lead past, the bedlam in the stands subsided like the sound of a fading siren. In disbelief and amazement, fans and horsemen alike stood spellbound at the sight of The Admiral taking another horse's dust.

Barely into the backstretch, Charley Kurtsinger went to the whip again, and War Admiral answered with a surge of power that whittled a foot or more from Seabiscuit's lead at every stride. Instantly, the crowd was on its feet again, shouting, yelling, and cheering on the favorite. And with every stride the cheering rose in pitch and volume. It reached bedlam height when, half way up the backstretch, War Admiral drew even, and for a moment the black nose passed the bay.

But it was only for a moment. Matching stride for stride, the two Man o' War colts — finest son and outcast grandson — flew down the backstretch and into the far turn as though they were yoked together, neither one giving or taking an inch. From the bleachers, stands, and clubhouse, the cheering rose to a tumultuous roar; railbirds, fans, and horsemen sensing that the two champions were equal in speed, that this was a battle of nerves and courage.

144

Around the turn the two came shoulder to shoulder. Against the rail, Georgie Woolf crouched low above Seabiscuit's neck, striding long in the stirrups, and urging him on with his voice. On the outside, Charley Kurtsinger drove with the whip, swinging it at every stride as they turned into the homestretch. There Seabiscuit's ears snapped back, and at a clip of Georgie's whip he turned on everything he had. In trying to meet the bid, Charley lashed with all the strength of his arm, but War Admiral had nothing left to give.

With wild cheering from the crowd spurring him on, Seabiscuit stormed down the homestretch like a tornado. At the eighth pole he was two lengths in the lead; at the sixteenth, two and a half. Then, with his ears up and Georgie standing in the stirrups, he galloped under the wire, winner by a full four lengths.

Horses, above all other animals, have the ability to win the love and admiration of humans. And emotions are seldom more violently stirred than when we see those we love engage in a desperate struggle. It is little wonder that the own-folks of both Seabiscuit and War Admiral were stirred to tears of joy or sorrow — not for themselves, but for the horses they loved like children.

Sam Riddle, one of the most noble sportsmen that American horse racing has ever known, stood with his glasses fixed untremblingly on War Admiral until the greatest joy and pride of his old age had passed

under the wire, a dethroned champion. For a moment he forced a smile to his lips, and bowed in acknowledgment of defeat toward the Howard box. Then, with his chin jutting belligerently, but with tears in his eyes, he turned without a word and left the clubhouse. And as throngs pressed around to congratulate the Howards on their way to the winner's circle, tears of joy and affection poured down Mrs. Howard's cheeks.

The horses were barely under the wire before thousands of shouting, cheering fans leaped the fences and poured onto the track — each one, regardless of which he had bet on, determined to get a closer look at Seabiscuit; the wonder horse, the champion of champions. Reporters, radio commentators, and photographers were waiting at the winner's circle, each frantic to get the first picture of the champion; the first interview with his jockey, his owners, and his trainer. War Admiral, the one-to-four favorite two minutes ago, was as forgotten as if he'd died when he was a foal. Only those reporters who couldn't get close to the winner's circle were waiting for him when Charley Kurtsinger rode him back to the scales. And there were tears in the Flying Dutchman's eyes as he slid from the saddle. "I have no excuses," he told the waiting reporters. "What else can I say; we just couldn't make it."

There were no tears in Georgie Woolf's eyes. A radiant smile was on his face as he rode Seabiscuit back to the circle, and his first words were not for the reporters, but for Tom Smith, "Gee, I sure wish Red could have rode this race today — instead of me."

"Yeah, but I kinda think the redhead was ridin' along with you, Georgie," Tom told him, and for a moment he forgot to hide his pride and happiness behind his usual mask of taciturnity.

It was only for a moment, though. When reporters tried to flatter him by calling him the greatest trainer in the world, and pressed him for his secret in converting a gimpy outcast into a world's champion, he would only say, "Seabiscuit ran just the way we trained him. I said before the race he was the best horse, and this decides it; there can't be any excuses, not for either horse."

Georgie Woolf's answer to the sports writers was a bit longer than Tom's, but just as much to the point. "I heard the crowd yelling when the Admiral caught up to us on the backstretch, but what they didn't know was that I let him catch up. The Biscuit runs best when some horse is driving him. Kurtsinger was really driving, but Biscuit was going easy. Around the turn he was looking War Admiral in the eye, and the Admiral was looking him back, but I knew it wouldn't last. Then I saw Biscuit pin back his ears and knew the question of the Admiral's gameness was going to be decided within the next few seconds. Suddenly I saw the tongue dart sidewise out of the corner of his mouth; the sign of defeat. It was the time to let Biscuit have his head and I let him go."

Although Georgie didn't say he had ridden the race exactly as Red had advised him to, he showed his appreciation by sending the redhead $1500, half of the double winner's fee Mr. Howard paid him for the race.

All who saw the race recognized it as being more a test of courage than of speed, even though Seabiscuit nearly broke the world's record for the distance. Not only in this country but in England, sports writers hailed it as the most courageous race ever run on an American track. With the Florida winter season opening soon, Mr. Howard was deluged with demands that he bring his "wonder horse" there to run in the $50,000 Widener Handicap. Every big track in the South was anxious to put up at least a $50,000 purse for a rematch between Seabiscuit and War Admiral, but neither owner was interested.

For Seabiscuit, there were only two great honors left to be won: the Santa Anita Handicap and Champion Money-winner of All-time. Both appeared to be easily within his reach, for no horse in the world could beat him unless given an unreasonable advantage, and he was already within $36,000 of Sun Beau's record. A win in the Santa Anita classic would put him far, far beyond it. Mr. Howard decided to return him to California, give him a long winter's rest, then retire him from racing after he had won the coveted classic.

9

As ALWAYS, Seabiscuit became as fat as a contented pig during his idleness. But when, in January 1939, Tom Smith and Georgie Woolf put him back into training, he rounded into marvelous condition, and was never more edgy for a race. With the Santa Anita Handicap only a month away, Tom thought it best to put him into an easy tightening-up race; one where he wouldn't have to strain himself to win. He chose a little purse race, to be run on Valentine's Day, and entered both Seabiscuit and Kayak II, a South American colt that Mr. Howard had recently imported.

There were only four horses entered in the Valentine's Day race, and Tom Smith's greatest interest was in finding out what Kayak could do in a race with such a horse as Seabiscuit. But it wasn't the South American colt that furnished the competition; it was Today, a rank outsider. For the first three-quarters of a mile, Today set a sizzling pace, and Georgie Woolf held Seabiscuit a length behind. At the far turn Georgie pulled up beside the tiring leader, then let Biscuit have his head for making his whirlwind stretch run. He had barely started when there was a sharp cracking sound, and the rhythm of his gait stuttered for an instant. Woolf immediately slowed him, but even under hard restraint, Biscuit drove on to take second place, while Kayak trailed far behind.

Nothing is more dangerous to an injured foreleg than to stop a running horse quickly, so Georgie slowed for a furlong before pulling to a full stop. There he slid from the saddle while Seabiscuit stood bobbing his head, his left forefoot barely touching the ground. The violent bobbing of a horse's head is a sure sign of tremendous pain, and at every track a horse ambulance is kept in readiness. The moment the champion came to a stop the ambulance driver started onto the track, but Tom Smith waved him back. He knew the pride of his horse too well for that — and within two minutes Seabiscuit had proved him right. He took two limping steps as Georgie Woolf led him toward the scales, stopped, raised his head, and looked at the awestruck crowd in the stands. Then, to cheering that could have been heard for miles, he walked on without the slightest sign of a limp.

But after reaching the privacy of his own stall he could hardly touch his foot to the floor.

Again the Sun Beau jinx had raised its head. Tom Smith made a careful examination, and tried to swallow the lump in his throat. The injury was beyond even his magic; a ruptured suspensory ligament in the left ankle. And no horse had ever raced successfully again after badly rupturing a suspensory ligament. There was only one thing to be done: Son would have to be retired from the track. To see him go when he was on the very threshold of everlasting greatness was heartbreaking to his own-folks, his millions of fans, and every horse lover in the country, but he wouldn't go without honors galore: the only horse beside Man o' War to have defeated a Triple Crown winner in a match race, highest money-winning four-year-old and five-year-old in the history of racing; top money-winner of all ages in one year, and second highest money-winner of all time.

Ever since Tom Smith had brought Seabiscuit from an ill-tempered, gimpy-legged outcast to a tractable and consistent winner, he had been recognized as one of the most skillful trainers in the United States. Some horsemen had gone so far as to call him a magician. In the three weeks between the time of Seabiscuit's injury and the running of the Santa Anita Handicap he came amazingly close to proving them right. With Seabiscuit out of the classic, his leg so sore and swollen that he couldn't be moved, Tom had to divide his time between doctoring Son and training Kayak into condition to take his place. How well he succeeded is a matter of racing history: Kayak won the classic, and by the day it was run Seabiscuit could again walk without limping.

For three years Mrs. Howard's heart had been set on winning the Santa Anita Handicap, but when Kayak won it she found the honor empty. In the past year she had come to yearn for it, not for herself, but for the courageous little horse that had come so close to winning it twice, and each time had lost by a nose through no fault of his own. When, at the end of March, Seabiscuit was retired to the Howard ranch near Willits, California, she decided to make the family home there — and Red Pollard was considered one of the family. Up and hobbling around on crutches, he started for the ranch as soon as the doctors would release him from the hospital. When they warned him that he must never mount a horse again, that his patched-up leg wouldn't stand the strain, he grinned and told them, "Then I reckon I'll have to find somebody to boost me up, 'cause Baby and me, we're still goin' places."

No finer place could have been found for Red and Seabiscuit to recuperate than the Howard ranch. Through the warm days of spring they were constantly together, Red swinging himself out to the paddock on his crutches each morning and afternoon, talking to his old friend as if he were another person, and telling him they were still going places together. But Red no longer called him Baby. Now he was "Pappy," for Fair Knightess and six other excellent mares would bear his colts before another spring.

Red's talks with Pappy were no secret to the owners and racing officials who came to visit at the ranch. And the sight of the two broken-down old campaigners, trying to comfort each other, brought many a lump into their throats, for the odds were a hundred to one that neither would know the feel of a saddle again. But they were wrong. Within a month Red was being boosted into a saddle on Pappy's back, and the two old friends were wandering around the fields together.

Faith, courage, and affection are the most potent healers the world has ever known, and on the Howard ranch all three were abundant. No day passed when Mr. and Mrs. Howard were at the ranch that they did not come to the stables to pet Pappy, and to encourage the boy who wouldn't give up his determination that "you and me, we're goin' places." And no expense was spared in making sure that both had the best medical care that doctors and veterinarians could provide.

Using a stock saddle, so as to put no strain on his own injured leg, and cautious never to put a strain on Pappy's, Red increased the length of his rides each day, and each day the gimpy legs grew stronger. By early summer they were traveling at an easy canter, and Red at last could walk without limping badly.

By early fall Red was letting Pappy take short bursts of speed where a meadow was level and springy under the hoof, but the rhythm of his gait was new. Through instinct or intelligence he had discovered a way of running that would take the greatest possible amount of stress off his weakened forelegs. And as he perfected the new gait his eagerness to run became almost uncontrollable. It was then that Mrs. Howard first noticed him standing in his stall with "the look of eagles in his eyes." Often he failed to see her coming with his evening carrot, but he would be standing with his head high, looking off into the distance as if he were seeing there a homestretch, and himself streaking down it toward the wire.

Most Thoroughbred stallions become haughty, proud, and intractable when they are used as sires, but Seabiscuit remained as gentle and affectionate as a kitten. It was not until the "look of eagles" came into his eyes that he became nervous and high-strung. Again he began walking his stall, and his urge to run became so keen that Red had trouble in holding him back. No horseman could fail to know that his battle spirit was up, that instinct told him he was in shape to race again, and that his idleness was driving him frantic.

In late October all Seabiscuit's own-folks gathered at the Howard ranch, where Tom Smith made a thorough examination of Pappy's legs and studied his new way of running. Miraculous as it seemed, the ruptured suspensory ligament had mended, tightened, and strengthened amazingly, and the new style of running relieved it of considerable strain. Tom believed that with careful training, designed to further strengthen the ligament and perfect the new gait, Son might be raced a few more times without too great risk of a crippling injury. With that assurance, all of Seabiscuit's own-folks felt that it would be unfair not to give him another chance to prove himself the greatest race horse of his time. It was decided that he should be put back into training, but that he would be permanently retired at the first sign of breaking down again.

When Mr. Howard announced that Seabiscuit would be put back into training, horsemen and sports writers throughout the country ridiculed the idea. They pointed out that, like heavyweight boxing champions, no Thoroughbred champion had ever made a successful comeback after once going into retirement, and that Seabiscuit would only become an object of public pity if he were allowed to race again. Track veterinarians were even more vehement. They insisted that a badly ruptured suspensory ligament could never be completely healed, and that if the champion were put into sufficiently stiff training to again prepare him for racing he would be hopelessly ruined. But Mr. Howard had more confidence in Tom Smith's judgment and in Seabiscuit's own instinct than in all the experts in the world. He decided that, in spite of all the risks, Seabiscuit should be given the chance he was so evidently yearning for.

With the decision made to return Seabiscuit to training, the first problem was to take weight off him, for since retirement he had gained nearly a hundred pounds. To relieve the strain on his legs, it must be taken off, but so carefully that his strength would not be impaired. Before leaving the ranch, Tom Smith prepared a special diet for him, and Red Pollard watched over it like a martinet. When he caught Ollie sneaking an extra ration into Pappy's stall, he ran him out of the barn with a pitchfork. From the day of the decision, Red was constantly with his old friend, massaging his legs with liniment, riding him morning and afternoon — heavily blanketed to sweat off weight — then leading him for an hour to cool him out thoroughly. And the walking was not for Seabiscuit's benefit alone. With every mile he walked, Red's own injured leg gained strength. It would never again be strong enough to endure the terrific strain of long training sessions on a racing pad, but Red was determined that by the time Pappy was again ready to race, he would be ready to stand in the stirrups.

At the end of November Red and Seabiscuit were moved to Santa Anita, and Tom Smith began his careful training, with Red at his side and Georgie Woolf in the saddle. For the first three weeks the workouts were light; simply a canter morning and afternoon to tighten up racing muscles and sweat off excess weight. By a week before Christmas, the weight was nearly down to racing form but Seabiscuit hadn't taken a lame step, was rounding into perfect physical condition, and was boiling over with eagerness to run. It was time to find out how much of his speed he had lost, and whether there was hope that he might successfully race again. When there was no one around the track, Tom had Georgie turn the aging old champ loose for three furlongs, and he left no doubt of his speed, covering the distance in thirty-four seconds — only a half second short of the world's record.

After such a showing Tom was anxious to begin sharp training, in order to build up Seabiscuit's stamina for longer distances, but it appeared that the Sun Beau jinx was still with him. The next day the winter rains set in, continuing every few days until the end of January. Tom dared to put Seabiscuit on the track only when it was sloppy enough not to pull at his hoofs. When it was heavy and sticky he had to be left in the stable, and every day he stood in his stall put fat back on his ribs.

At the beginning of February the weather cleared, the track dried, and Tom went back to regular training. But he had to start all over, cantering Son in a blanket to sweat off the fat. Not until the sixth could he be given another short speed trial, and then it fell a full second behind the time he had made in December. It was clear that he had become sluggish and needed the sharpening of racing competition, so Tom decided to start him in an unimportant seven-furlong race to be run on February 9, and to put Red on him. That would give him a chance to see whether or not either of them could really make a comeback.

When the news broke that Seabiscuit and Red were going to try to make their comeback in the little week-day race, their loyal fans took the day off, thronged the track, stormed the betting windows, and made Biscuit the short-odds favorite. But they went home shaking their heads sorrowfully. The best he had been able to do was a poor third.

The first real test for the Santa Anita Handicap was the San Carlos, to be run on the seventeenth. Tom decided to enter both Seabiscuit and Kayak in this warm-up race, though he had been unable to put either of them into sharp training for it. The result was heartbreaking to the fans, who had made the pair their odds-on favorites. Seabiscuit finished sixth in a field of nine, and Kayak was next to last. That time, the fans went home disillusioned: Poor old Seabiscuit! He was all washed up. It was a shame to put the poor old champ into races and let him disgrace himself. What was the matter with Charley Howard? Had he gone greedy for money? And what was the matter with Tom Smith? Had he lost his skill and judgment? Kayak, last year's winner of the Santa Anita, was evidently as washed up as Seabiscuit. Both of them ought to be withdrawn from the San Antonio Handicap and the classic.

The angry yapping of the fans was loud enough to reach Tom Smith's ears, and he paid as much attention to it as usual. He had been well satisfied with both races, and particularly with Red's riding. His bad leg had stood up to the strain in good shape, he hadn't been obliged to favor it by sitting flat, and he had shown no fear of getting in close to the rail. As for the horses, both had shown well for the amount of sharpening they'd had, and it would do them both good to have smelled a little dust.

10

WHILE the betting odds against Seabiscuit and Kayak mounted like a kite in a gale, Tom Smith went quietly about his training. Each morning he had his pupils on the track at dawn, and let the railbirds watch them in disgust as he put them through their paces. Then, in the late afternoon, he brought them out again, letting them sharpen each other in a burst of speed that would have sent the railbirds into a flutter if they'd been there with their stopwatches.

Even though the fans and railbirds had written off the Howard entries in the San Antonio, Webb Everett refused to do so, although he was somewhat doubtful about the seven-year-old Seabiscuit. Everett assigned him a weight of 124 pounds, and Kayak 129, but gave no one of eleven other starters more than 119. He proved to be a good judge of Tom Smith, but not so good in his rating of Seabiscuit. The old champ romped home, eased up, to equal the track record, beat Kayak by two and a half lengths, and put himself $10,000 nearer to Sun Beau's record.

The same fans who had grievingly written off "poor old Seabiscuit" nearly tore the stands down as he came winging toward them in the homestretch. Newspaper headlines blossomed from coast to coast, "Seabiscuit himself again!" "Old Iron Horse wins San Antonio in a breeze!" "Howard stable a cinch for Santa Anita Cap!"

Seabiscuit's win had been as glorious as unexpected, but it called down the wrath of the sports writers and railbirds on Tom Smith's head. They stormed at him for his secret workouts, claiming that they were simply a trick to increase the betting odds. For the first — and probably only — time in his life, Tom became talkative and gave away one of his training secrets. "You want to know the truth?" he asked Jack McDonald of the San Francisco *Call-Bulletin*. "If the clockers and the turf writers want to call me a heel, I can't help it. I've got nothing to hide and never have had. I don't work Seabiscuit out until late in the day to fool anybody but Seabiscuit himself.

"You see, Seabiscuit is a horse inclined to put on weight, more so than any horse I've ever trained. His legs would never stand the gaff of all the hard work required to keep him down to racing weight, so I have been forced to devise other methods for keeping his weight down. I do it by making him think he's going to race a lot of days when he isn't. On days when I throw a good hard work into him I take him out for a short blow early in the morning, just as if he was going to the post in the afternoon.

"After he's been breezed that way in the morning I put the blinkers and the bit where he can see them, and let him go without his feed. That puts him on edge. He thinks he's going to the post later in the day. He's keyed up all day like a jitterbug. All day long he's like that and just naturally frets off weight. Then, about five o'clock, I let him go out on the track and turn on the heat. He comes back relaxed, fit, and ready for the hay and oats."

Even though Tom might have fooled Seabiscuit, he hadn't fooled Webb Everett; the handicapper assigned the champ a load of 130 pounds to carry in the classic, weighted Kayak with 129, and gave no other starter above 118. The two Howard horses were combined as an entry in the mutuels, but in spite of the tremendous weight disadvantage the fans made them the six-to-five favorite — and their money was on the Old Iron Horse. As Maurice Bernard, a Los Angeles sports writer, put it, "It's the field against Seabiscuit, and Seabiscuit against Sun Beau, in the sixth running of the Santa Anita Handicap today. A record crowd of fans will be rooting for Charles S. Howard's old champ to dethrone Sun Beau as the leading money-winning Thoroughbred of all time. Yes, sir, Biscuit will have the moral backing of every man, woman and child. 'If my horse doesn't win it, I hope Seabiscuit does,' is the way rival owners and trainers feel about the world's richest race."

No horse race in the United States ever created as much excitement as that engendered by the 1940 Santa Anita Handicap, and it was entirely due to Seabiscuit's impressive winning of the San Antonio. Airline flights from the East Coast were flown in sections to accommodate the wealthy owners and sportsmen. Two special trains had to be run from San Francisco. From the entire West the fans were drawn to Los Angeles as steel filings are drawn to a magnet. Long before noon, twenty-two thousand automobiles jammed every parking space within a mile of the track. The movie studios were emptied, and Santa Anita Park was packed as tightly as pickles in a jar with fans, horse lovers, and racing enthusiasts — each with his fingers crossed for the hard-luck favorite and his equally hard-luck jockey. Atop the grandstand, and even atop the tote board, newsreel cameras were mounted, and the betting windows were mobbed.

Among the entire throng there was only one who wasn't watching excitedly as the horses started away for the post. That one was Mrs. Howard. She was back at the stables, waiting at Pappy's stall door, for she was afraid of breaking down completely if she were to see the race. She could only wait and pray, trying to convince herself that the charm of the St. Christopher's medal pinned to Red's silks would be strong enough to offset the Sun Beau jinx, for the old bugaboo had threatened to raise its head again — Seabiscuit had drawn stall thirteen in the starting gate. Though Mr. Howard tried to control his nerves, his voice trembled as he gave Red careful and detailed advice on strategy for riding the race.

Of all Seabiscuit's own-folks, the only two who showed no sign of jittery nerves were Tom Smith and Red Pollard. Neither had the slightest doubt of the outcome, so there was no reason to be nervous. They listened respectfully while Mr. Howard gave his advice, then as Tom led Son away toward the track, he looked up at Red, winked, and told him, "You know the horse and he knows you. Go out there and bring him in."

No jockey ever went out to ride in an important race with a greater handicap than Red Pollard took with him when he rode Seabiscuit onto the track. His injured leg was little bigger around than his arm, and a gnarled, purple welt ran the entire length of it. His doctor had made a special trip from Willits, to remove the bandages just before the race. He was convinced that the leg would hold up under the ordinary strain of racing, but with any severe pressure it might snap as easily as a matchstick.

As one after another of the fourteen starters in the

classic came onto the track there was a polite burst of clapping from the stands, but when Red rode Sea- biscuit from the paddock the cheering rose to a deafen- ing tumult. As if acknowledging the applause, the old campaigner stopped for a moment, looked the crowd over, then sauntered on calmly beside his old friend, Pumpkin, to the starting gate.

Red paid no more attention than Seabiscuit to the thunderous ovation. To him it was no more than the just due of the greatest horse that ever lived, and he had other things to think about. The least of them was not stall thirteen; not because it was supposed to be an unlucky number, but because it was next to the farthest starting position from the rail. A horse starting from that far out would have to gain nearly two extra lengths in crossing to the rail, just to stay even with the starter from the number-one stall — and Kayak had drawn stall number two.

Before reaching the post Red had his mind thor- oughly made up. He must get away to a flying start, then cross to the rail in front of the pack, rather than inside or behind it. There were two reasons for his decision. If he crossed behind the pack, Seabiscuit might be blocked, as Count Atlas had blocked him in the 1938 Classic. If they tried to cross inside the pack they might easily get into tight enough quarters that his own fragile leg would be bumped or squeezed enough to break it.

In the starting gate Seabiscuit stood calm but

poised, and Red crouched with his whip raised. At the bell he slapped it down, a signal to Pappy for the best he had. And he gave it. In a mighty leap, he shot from the stall and into full stride, then clamped his ears back and dug in. But he was not alone. Over against the rail, Wedding Call and Specify had broken lightning-fast, but Whichcee was storming up to take the lead from them. Crouching low, his mouth only inches behind Seabiscuit's flattened ears, Red talked him on. As they passed the wildly cheering grandstand crowd, they drew away from the thundering pack. There Red glanced back over his shoulder, just enough to make sure they were in the clear, then hurtled to the inside, gaining the rail close behind the three sprinting leaders.

On the clubhouse turn, Specify dropped out, and Wedding Call fell back more than a length, but Whichcee flew on, streaking around the bend and into the backstretch. Seabiscuit raced close at Whichcee's tail, with Wedding Call hanging on gamely, his head lapping Biscuit's hip. All the way up the backstretch and into the far turn, they held the dizzying pace so evenly that a single blanket might have covered all three. There, to the screeching, screaming plea of the fans, Red turned Seabiscuit loose to make his bid. But as he surged into his challenge his younger rivals surged to meet it; Whichcee still holding the lead, tight against the rail, and Wedding Call moving up on the outside.

With Seabiscuit in the
center, they fought on
around the end of the track
almost head-to-head. Then,
to stunned silence from the
crowd, Wedding Call drove
into the lead, bearing in
a little as they whirled
around the near turn and
into the homestretch. Just
what Red Pollard had
feared most had caught up
with them. They were in
close quarters. The space
between Whichcee and
Wedding Call was barely
wide enough to squeeze
through. If he held Sea-
biscuit back and tried to go
around, the race would certainly be lost. If he tried to
drive between, the chance
of breaking his own fragile
leg was at least fifty-fifty.
It was then that Doug Dod-
son, Wedding Call's jockey,
heard Red praying aloud.
An instant later his whip
slashed down, and Seabis-

cuit shot through the narrow gap as though he'd been struck by a lightning shaft.

As if the same shaft had struck the grandstand, the crowd leaped to its feet, shrieking and yelling, *"Come on Seabiscuit! Come on Seabiscuit!"*

And Seabiscuit came on.

To cheering such as no race track on earth had ever heard, he came on and on. At the sixteenth pole the race was over. Wedding Call had dropped out of contention, and Kayak was coming up strongly to overhaul the tiring Whichcee and take second place. Red took Seabiscuit to the rail and let him breeze on under the wire, his stride easy and rhythmic, and his ears wigwagging signals to the crowd. Still the superb showman, he was telling his friends up there in the stands that there had been nothing to it.

But there had been. In that one slash of his whip, Red Pollard had lifted Seabiscuit to the championship of the world — more than $60,000 ahead of Sun Beau's record. And he had lifted Mr. and Mrs. Howard, to say nothing of himself and Tom Smith, into the greatest joy of their lives. No one could say that the old campaigner hadn't finished like a true champion, for, eased up as he had been during the last half furlong, he had broken the track record set by Kayak the year before, carrying his 130 pounds a mile and a quarter in two minutes, one and one-fifth seconds. Only once in American turf history had that time been bettered;

170

when Sarazen, carrying 120 pounds, stopped the watches two-fifths of a second sooner.

Reporters who were at Santa Anita that memorable day say the fans went literally crazy with joy, swept out of all reason at the sight of something they had hoped to see but thought they never would. Thousands of people were actually crying when Seabiscuit and Red came back to the winner's circle. Some were sobbing during the race, when it seemed that Seabiscuit and Red had been cut off and would be cheated out of another winning of the classic through hard luck.

Reporters, photographers, and newsreel men crowded to catch the first pictures, the first words from the joyful redhead. But Red's first words were not for them; they were for Mrs. Howard, as she came hurrying from the stable, smiling happily through her tears. "I hit him at the head of the stretch," he told her. "I had to, but he understood. It was our last trip, and we had to make it a good one."

Mr. Howard was more jubilant when he hurried from the clubhouse. "It was perfect!" he told the reporters. "It was the greatest thrill of my life! I got ten times as much kick out of this win as I did from Seabiscuit's victory over War Admiral. Will I race him again? Well, we haven't decided as yet, although Seabiscuit is sound and likes to race more than anything else. I may keep him here for the

Hollywood Gold Cup, but that's something that still must be decided."

Tom Smith, the man who had found Seabiscuit, transformed him from an outcast into the world's champion, and loved him enough to call him Son, had a different opinion. "Of course, it's up to Mr. Howard," he told the reporters, "but if I owned the horse I wouldn't race him again. He's done enough. What's left for him to do?"

A few days later, Seabiscuit, as contented as though he understood and agreed with Tom, went back to spend the rest of his life being Pappy to a growing family of sons and daughters on the Howard ranch. A year later he made another trip to Santa Anita; this time for the unveiling of the life-sized bronze statue of himself that stands in the paddock there. But it was not a triumph for him alone. All his own-folks were there to share in his honor, and they all belonged there, for without their love and understanding he might well have remained a forgotten outcast. No finer tribute could have been paid to the valiant old warrior than that inscribed on the medal awarded him, "The main issue in life is not the victory but the fight; the essential thing is not to have won but to have fought well."